FAITH

SPIRITUAL ARCHITECTURE

FAITH

SPIRITUAL ARCHITECTURE

LOFT

SPIRITUAL ARCHITECTURE. NEW RELIGIOUS BUILDINGS

Editorial Coordinator and texts: Cristina Paredes Benítez
Art Director: Mireia Casanovas Soley
Design and layout coordination: Claudia Martínez Alonso
Layout: Esperanza Escudero

© 2009 Loft Publications
LOFT Publications
Via Laietana, 32 4.° Of. 92
08003 Barcelona, Spain
T +34 932 688 088
F +34 932 687 073
loft@loftpublications.com
www.loftpublications.com

ISBN: 978-84-96936-35-5

Printed in Spain by Egedsa

ONTENTS

INTRODUCTION

During the making of this book, many questions arose regarding what is 'holy', what religion means and the important role religious architecture has played throughout history. All civilizations have developed cults and diverse religions. We only have to mention two extremely well-known examples, i.e., the Egyptian and Greek civilizations, to see the practically inevitable relationship between civilization and religion. Why has mankind been raising buildings to honor gods since ancient times? What makes a construction holy? Answering these questions would require various volumes and the participation of anthropologists, theologians and historians — and even then many questions would probably still need to be settled. The special relationship between architecture and religion is far-reaching and dates from prehistoric formations and alignments of large rocks through to Roman temples and Egyptian pyramids on to the splendid churches of the Italian Renaissance. Even if one is not particularly religious, the legacy that religions convey to its culture is undeniable.

Power, closely linked to religion, has used religious architecture for its own benefit. Governors and other powerful figures over the centuries financed the construction of religious buildings to disseminate beliefs but also to legitimize their power or atone for their sins. Some constructions were made possible thanks to donations from the faithful, such as the Sagrada Familia in Barcelona, built by Antoni Gaudí, which underlines the popular nature of all religions.

Religious buildings are often perceived as closed spaces anchored in the past, but when they distance themselves from traditional dogmatic structures, offering free spaces for the interpretation of spiritual affairs, they can become modern and open places that promote dialogue and understanding among believers. Today, in the Western world particularly, there appears to be a process of laicism that could lead one to think that religious architecture is falling into disuse. However, the truth is that figures speak to a rise in religious practices, and in countries such as China and Russia, religion cannot be denied. This is forcing architects to rethink the uses and functions of new churches and temples and to bear in mind the social changes related with different sects.

Religious buildings should satisfy a number of particular specifications of a functional nature, such as materials, acoustics, spaces for holding different liturgies, etc. Moreover, they must also meet a number of symbolic requirements. Spiritual architecture, like music, images and prayers, contributes to providing another dimension to the religious experience, to finding peace or a moral path. In this volume we present diverse buildings, including small chapels, large temples where different cults can meet and mediation spaces, which are all places for worship and reflection and which also help shore up the concepts of community and group.

Defining the concept of religion inevitably creates controversy. The religious phenomenon can manifest itself in different ways, depending on beliefs and the groups that express them. Its structure may be very diverse: some religions are rigidly organized and others may be integrated within the culture of a society. In fact, the word 'religion' is used as a synonym for organized religion, i.e., one accepted by a particular society. This has the effect that a set of tenets recognized as a religion in one place may not be considered as such somewhere else. The dictionary defines religion as a 'set of beliefs or dogma regarding a deity, feelings of veneration and fear toward this divinity, moral standards for individual and social behavior and ritualized practices, principally prayer and sacrifice to worship the supreme being".

From the anthropological viewpoint, religion unites elements such as tradition, history, mythology, faith and beliefs, liturgies and prayers, mystical experiences, etc. It is a discipline that raises the question of whether religious manifestations are linked to the continuation of humanity, i.e., whether they constitute an essential phenomenon of mankind. Independently of the answer, the fact is that religions have always been present in our societies and continue to be so today.

Religions can be classified in different manners, the main ones being by theological concept and origin. Theological concept refers to the belief in the existence of one or various gods (monotheism or polytheism) or whether deities are considered as a metaphoric recourse. Religions are classified into families in line with their origin: Abrahamic (or Semitic), Dharmic (or Indic), Iranian, neo-pagan, traditional, etc. The purpose of this book is not to make an exhaustive list of contemporary religions, although it is interesting to have a general idea. Below is a list of some of the main religions and others which have derived from them, followed by a brief explanation of the features of the beliefs related to the projects that feature in this work.

- Islam
  - Shi'a
  - Sunni
- Sufism
- Judaism
  - Secular
  - Orthodox
- Christianity
  - Catholic Church
  - Orthodox church
  - Coptic Church
  - Eastern Catholic Churches
  - Protestantism
    · Lutheranism
    · Baptist
    · Presbyterian
    · Evangelist
    · Methodist
    · Reformed Christians
    · Quakers
    · Universalists
    · United Church of Christ
    · Adventists
    · Anglicans
  - Jehovah's Witnesses
  - Mormonism
  - Worldwide Church of God
  - Ecumenism

- Buddhism
  - Theravāda
  - Mahāyāna
  - Vajrayāna
- Hinduism
  - Shivaism
  - Vaishnavism
  - Advaita Vedanta
- Indigenous
  - Animism
  - Witchcraft
  - Shamanism
  - Fetishism
  - Totemism
  - Australian
  - American
  - African
    · Yoruba
    · Voodoo
    · Santeria
    · Candomblé
    · Quimbanda
    · Umbanda
  - Asian
- Jainism
- Shinto
- Sikh
- Taoism
- Zoroastrianism

ISLAM

Islam involves a number of tenets and teachings that constitute religion of the Muslims. It originated with the Prophet Mohammed, o in the 7th century predicted the revelations of God, or Allah. The of these successive revelations are set out in the holy book, the an, which establishes that there is no god except Allah and Mommed is his messenger. Islam forms part of the Abrahamic onotheistic religions founded by the descendents of Abraham and rships Allah exclusively. Unlike Christianity, which defends the canon he Trinity, Islam holds with the uniqueness of God. It also coincides h Judaism in the incomparable and unrepresentable nature of the d: the Muslim religion accepts no representations of God in images. well as the Koran, there are other texts that form the historical ord of the actions and teachings of the Prophet, i.e., the Hadith and Sunnah. Islam admits the Torah, the Books of Solomon and the spel as holy books.

The dissemination of Islam was really fast. Barely a century after death of Mohammed it had already reached the Atlantic in one di-tion and the boundaries of China in the other. Between the 9th and h centuries, the Islamic civilization developed an important culture d Muslims were responsible for major advances in philosophy and natural sciences. A later development of the religion, which began lowing the death of Mohammed, gave rise to different doctrines de-nding on whether or not particular dogmas were accepted: they in-de the Sunni, Shi'a and Sufi denominations.

The main Islamic beliefs are: God is eternal, magnificent, om-potent, omnipresent, creator and unique. Muslims also believe in e angels, the mission of the prophets, resurrection and a future life er the Final Judgment. Muslims have five duties: as well as the pro-sion of the faith, these are prayer (which should be done five times a), the compulsory alms for the poor (zakat), fasting during Ramadan d the pilgrimage to Mecca at least once in a lifetime.

CHRISTIANITY

The origins of Christianity must be sought in the life and works of sus, which extended throughout his life, death and resurrection. urches that consider themselves followers of Jesus of Nazareth form rt of the Christian religion. Historically it arose from Judaism, when sus was identified as the Messiah announced in the Old Testament. is ambivalent relationship with Judaism is one of its major charac-istics, although it can sometimes be difficult to describe. Christianity included in the monotheistic religions and, together with Judaism, am and Zoroastrianism, is one of the faiths that claim to possess a storical revelation. Christianity is based on uplifting historical facts with a view to the salvation of mankind. God in Jesus Christ reconciles men with themselves, permitting them to reach fullness beyond the human scope (Heaven). The fact that Emperor Constantine adopted Christianity as the official religion of the Roman Empire in the year 313 made a powerful contribution to the dissemination of the religion. Cen-turies later, the Christian character of the West determined the expan-sion of this cult in America and parts of Asia, and later in Africa. Al-though Christianity is a religion with a universalist vocation, it has been unable to prevent the appearance of internal factions which dissented from the organization and liturgy of the Church. Some of the differ-ences that developed between the 9th and 11th centuries led to the Eastern Schism, which saw the separation between the Christian Church of the West and East. The 16th century Reformation was the ex-pression of reformist attitudes in the Church. These dogmatic and practical differences therefore separate the three large families of Chris-tianity, i.e., Catholic, Orthodox and Protestant (which in turn gathers to-gether a wide variety of ecclesiastical denominations and differences).

CATHOLICISM

The Catholic dogmas are the beliefs that identify and differentiate Catholicism from other Christian confessions. They are based on the Bible and the apostolic traditions, unlike the Hebrews, who base part of their beliefs on the Old Testament. Some of the most important creeds are the Holy Trinity, the Eucharist (the bread and wine turned into the body and blood of Christ), and the existence of Purgatory, the Immacu-late Conception and the Assumption of the Virgin. Catholics also rec-ognize seven sacraments, including ones that involve Christian initia-tion (baptism, communion and confirmation), healing (penitence or confession and the anointing of the sick) and finally, services to the community (the sacrament of marriage and of the apostolic ministry).

Catholics also have the Ten Commandments, which can be sum-marized in one: you shall love God above all else and your neighbor as yourself. There are five rules in the Catholic Church: to hear mass on Sunday and important feast days; to confess your mortal sins are least once a year and before communion; to take communion at least at Easter; to fast and abstain from eating meat when the Church so dic-tates and to help it in its needs. The most important feasts are Christ-mas Day, celebrating the birth of Jesus, and Easter, which commemo-rates His passion, death and resurrection.

PROTESTANTISM

Protestantism refers to the collection of Christian religions that arose from the 16th century Reformation or which were influenced by it. The intention of Protestants was not to create a new church, but to reform the existing one and to return to the doctrines and apostolic

practices. Despite the aspiration to not break with the Church of Rome, separation did occur in the end. The ideas of Erasmus of Rotterdam influenced one of the early reformists, Luther. Luther's complaints against Papal indulgences and his criticism of the religious rituals of the time saw the start of the Reformist movements and even led to them being classified as heresy. Calvin was another leading figure behind Protestantism. Influenced by Luther, he shared with him the negation of the authority of the Church of Rome and denied apostolic succession from the apostle Peter. He also gave a great deal of importance to the Bible as the only rule of faith and conduct. The invention of the printing press facilitated the dissemination of Reformist ideas. Luther translated the bible into German to make it more accessible to the people and to erode the influence of the ecclesiastic hierarchy and the priests. Protestantism expanded across northern Europe, particularly in the West. However, most of the continent upheld the beliefs of the Catholics, who reaffirmed their doctrines at the Council of Trent. There was to later be a separation between the different Protestant churches, although they all have elements in common. The Anglican Church, for example, was not initially influenced by Protestantism, although its subsequent rupture with Rome brought it clearly closer to the Reformed Church.

Protestants emphasize the glory and absolute transcendence of God and proclaim the authority of the Bible. Protestants have always promoted versions of this holy text in the languages of different countries and they value the word of the Bible above liturgical ceremonies, which they consider excessive. Protestants conserve only two sacraments, i.e., baptism and the Holy Feast, and their priests do not have to take a vow of chastity.

EVANGELICAL CHURCH

There are various churches within Protestantism, including the Evangelic Church, which in turn includes Lutherans, Calvinists, Presbyterians, Baptists and Methodists. Beyond their differences, they share a common doctrine based on the Bible as the only rule of faith and conduct. Their practice involves a return to the liturgical simplicity of the primitive church and consists of the public reading of the Bible, homily, the celebration of the Feast, prayer and community song.

BAPTIST CHURCH

One of the main 'free' or 'non-conformist' Protestant churches, its main feature is baptism by immersion. The Baptist Church was founded in England circa 1612 by Thomas Helwys, the first person to defend the right to religious freedom. The Baptists were to later begin in the United States, where the religion spread quickly. The Bible is a Baptist's only rule of faith and conduct. They believe a personal religious experience or conversion is needed to be able to form part of the

Church as the mystical body of Christ. Their churches are local, autonomous and with their own governments, and although they come together to try to achieve particular goals, they do not have a single and common authority. They support the separation of Church and State and religious freedom for all men and they practice two ordinances, i.e., baptism (always of believers and by immersion) and communion. There are two trends, one in favor of the thesis of the Ecumenical movement and the other against it.

PRESBYTERIAN CHURCH

A movement within Protestantism that upholds the form of ecclesiastical organization developed by Calvin and other 16th-century reformers. According to its doctrine, Christ is the only head of the Church and all members are equal. Three levels are established in its organization: community or parish, in which the organization is run by a council headed by a pastor; synod, formed by the pastors in a region and an elder for each parish; and, finally, the general assembly, a group comprising the same number of parishioners and elders as which govern the parish churches. Liturgical acts are extremely simple, involving only song, reading and Bible study and prayer. Baptism is offered to children and communion is relatively infrequent.

ECUMENISM

Ecumenism is a movement that exists in practically all Christian churches. Its goal is to reestablish the unity that Christ desired for His church. From this movement of renovation comes an optimistic attitude and vision of the world and mankind. The Ecumenical movement shares an ideology and even an organization, although this is not its purpose: Ecumenists believe in the possibility of the union of the Christian churches and, were their definitive union to happen, Ecumenism would disappear.

This movement of biblical, liturgical, theological and pastoral renewal led to a change of attitude within the Catholic Church at Vatican II, particularly in terms of acceptance of religious freedom and the ecclesiastical nature of the different Christian confessions. Despite these signs of rapprochement, the unity of Christian religions appears to still be a long way off. Disagreements between the patriarchal practices of the Orthodox Church and the ambiguous relationship between it and the other confessions also make understanding more difficult.

JUDAISM

The religion of the Jews, founded by Abraham. In the face of the polytheism of neighboring communities, the people of Israel were chosen to receive and disseminate the revealed truth of a single God. In Judaism, God is defined as an inspirational and sovereign being, create

from nothing, holy, just, all-knowing and omnipotent. Jehovah created the world in an act of goodness and man reflects this divine freedom. This freedom involves man's responsibility with respect to his actions, which is why rewards and punishment are also given out in earthly life. The pact between Jehovah and man involves God's protection of his ally in exchange for imposing a sign upon him, i.e., circumcision, and subjecting him to His law. The covenant will be completed with the arrival of the Messiah, the descendent of David.

The Jews consecrated Israel as the Holy Land and began to differentiate Israel from the rest of the world (Diaspora). The synagogues, which substitute the temple of Jerusalem, face Israel and prayers and celebrations coincide with its climate and seasons.

The Law, explained in the Pentateuch or Torah, constitutes the only and totalitarian code that contains the main texts of Judaism. As well as the law written in the Torah and the other texts of the Old Testament, there are oral teachings called Talmud, considered to be complementary. Feast days in Judaism begin at sunset the evening before. One of the best known is the Sabbath, i.e., the ban on working on Saturdays, exceeded in solemnity only by the Day of Atonement, or Yom Kippur. The destruction of the temple of Jerusalem in 70 A.D. produced a substantial change in the religious group, with worship involving sacrifices disappearing to be replaced by prayer. The liturgy prescribes three daily prayers: dawn, midday and evening. Feast days feature a fourth prayer in the mid-morning and a fifth is added at Yom Kippur.

The main Jewish symbols are the Star of David — said to have been adopted on his war shield although its current significance was given after the Middle Ages — and the seven-armed candelabra called the Menorah.

BUDDHISM

The Western term that defines the beliefs and practices centered on Buddha and His teachings. As with many other religions, Buddhism was originally a single set of beliefs which began to disintegrate due to different interpretations of the initial doctrine and its capacity for adaption to the cultures where it spread. It is not a religion resulting from divine revelation, nor which proclaims the existence of a God. The teachings are not considered dogmas or beliefs, and believers are even encouraged to question them for enhanced understanding.

Buddha means "He who has awakened" and Buddhist teachings are aimed at the awakening of man and the discovery of the infinite chain of causes that form the world. It particularly involves principles of human, individual and social ethics. The nucleus of the doctrine is centred on the four noble truths: first, suffering is universal; second, its cause is desire; third, desire has to be suppressed to end pain; and fourth, the road toward the suppression of desire is the 'eightfold path'.

Practice should be individual and language is used only as a guide. The eightfold path comprises straight comprehension, straight intention, straight word, straight action, straight means of existence, straight effort and straight attention and concentration. Buddhism does not believe in a permanent soul that transmigrates from an earthly existence to a divine one, but in five qualities (the form or body; feelings; perception; mental formations and conscience) all in constant flux. According to Buddhism, life is a continual flow of changing shapes, where everything happens according to karma, i.e., the law of causality. The individual follows his or her process of moral progress to reach nirvana or the definitive liberation from rebirth and therefore suffering. In Buddhism, rebirth does not signify reincarnation and meditation is one of the basic tools in the search for nirvana.

Buddhism developed from the teachings the prince or nobleman Siddhartha Gautama, known as The Buddha, disseminated circa 500 B.C., in the northeast of India. Between 300 B.C. and 700 A.D. it became the main religion of the country. Although it was on the point of disappearing from there by around the 13th century, it had already spread right across Asia.

The life of Siddhartha is used as an example and guide for followers in their spiritual search. Tradition has it that after the death of Buddha, a council met to establish the doctrine and monastic discipline to follow. A century later, differences regarding the meaning of the doctrine led to the creation of two tendencies: one which defended tradition and monastic life, the Theravāda, and another, more liberal one, which led to the Mahāyāna school. The traditional Theravāda school bases its faith on the historic Buddha, His teachings and the community. The Mahāyāna school is based on the writings of the Sanskrit tradition and believes in the need for Buddhism's evolution. A third school, which arose from Mahāyāna, is Vajrayāna, based on ritualistic meditations, gesture and sexual symbolism. The decentralization of Buddhism by different countries and its adaptation to local religions has generated a great flexibility of points of view and focuses, although a number of common principles are maintained.

SACRED HEART PARISH CENTER

Lamott Architekten | Völklingen-Ludweiler, Germany | 2001
© Werner Huthmacher

Religion: Catholic

The town where this parish center is located is in a mining area famous for its old foundry. In 1996 it was decided to replace the old community center, which had to be knocked down because of the settlement of the foundations. The new location on the outskirts of town is in an area where there is a retirement home, school and single-family properties.

The lack of architectural definition and the stylistic diversity of the buildings led to the design of a construction which would generate contrast instead of one that would blend in with the neighborhood. In this way, the design also gives the center a marked personality. It fans around a courtyard shared by the church and the other parish buildings.

The courtyard has been elevated above street level to unite all the spaces in the parish complex, including the church, youth club, auditorium, kindergarten, administrative offices and rectory. The roof unifies the spaces and four concrete slabs symbolically define the central courtyard. The biggest, lying over a pool, symbolizes the threshold that leads inside the church. A small bridge crosses the pond, a healing and purifying element.

A number of passages from the Revelation of St. John which mark the church entrance have been engraved on the door. The cross is outside, surrounded by a corten steel facade to make it inaccessible, although it can be seen from inside thanks to the glass walls. This symbolizes the ceremonies and prayers inside the church penetrating the walls to radiate outside.

Location map

Floor plan, parish center

0   3   6

^   Simplicity and minimalism are notable through the shapes of the buildings, the finishes and the choice of materials.

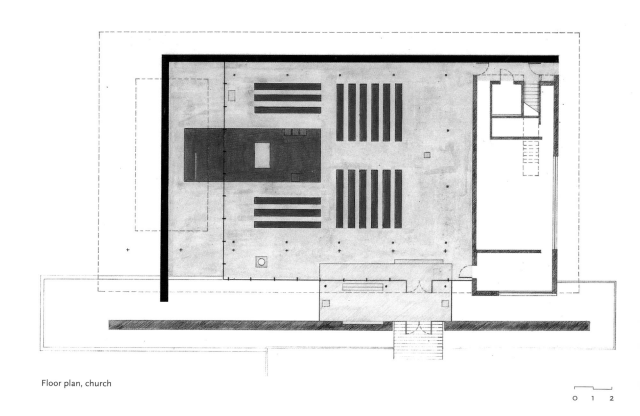

Floor plan, church

0　1　2

Sections

The architects say the lack of images inside the church is an image in itself. Here it is materials that define the space and produce a spiritual atmosphere.

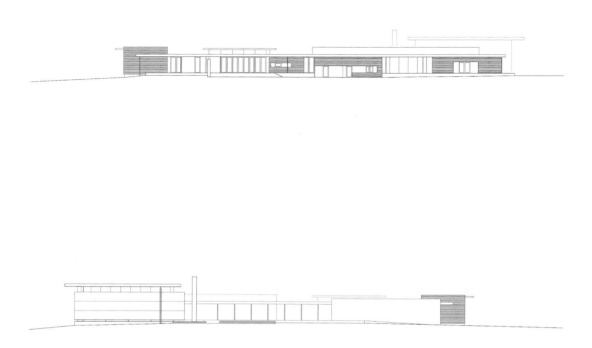

Elevations

VIIKKI CHURCH

JKMM Architects | Helsinki, Finland | 2005
© Jussi Tiainen, Arno de la Chapelle, Kimo Räisänen

Religion: Lutheran

This church is the central element of a larger urban-development project which will be carried out gradually. It extends across a space among various buildings between a park and a market. The relationship between the church and its environ will be defined on the basis of the draft plan the team at JKMM Architects made for the tender called to decide the design of the church.

The architectural decisions bore the prefabrication concept in mind. In fact, prefabricated pieces were used in the construction and the building was reinforced. A number of insulating exterior walls were added to the pillars and the Glulam wood beams on the ceiling — laminated and pasted wood — were reinforced with panels. The interior covering of spruce boards was treated with bleach to facilitate cleaning and renovation. The acoustic details of the false ceiling are made from compressed plywood elements.

The style of this church recalls the impressions left by the Finnish forest: an image of nature and spirituality. The architects also designed the pillar structures and beams with the idea of creating an atmosphere that would lift the spirits thanks to the use of wood. The architects created the pews, furniture and lamps to satisfy the requirements of the church and its parish center. The church combines modern and traditional construction methods, as well as rustic and sophisticated surfaces. In short, it is a building that reworks the tradition of wood churches and includes ecological criteria in building.

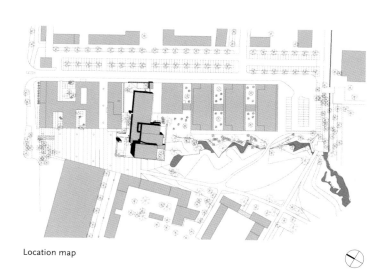

Location map

Longitudinal section

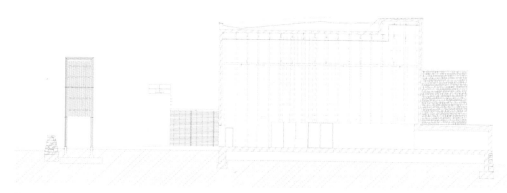

Cross-section

South elevation

Elevation of the church and parish center from the square

The church facade, made from untreated materials to give it an aged look, has been covered with alamo wooden boards and side coverings formed of assembled horizontal floorboards.

∧ Warm wood envelops the whole of the church interior. The altar furniture contrasts with the silver altarpiece, whose burgundy tones change whe the light hits it.

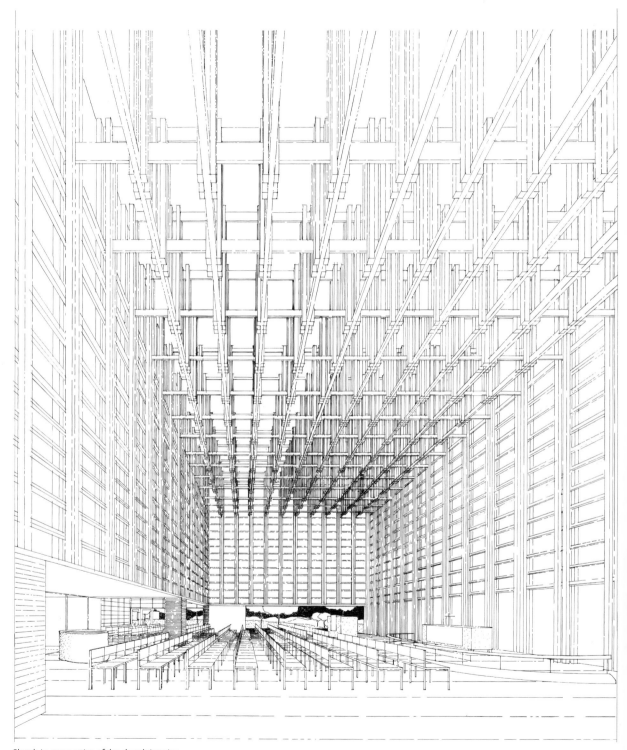

Sketch in perspective of the church interior

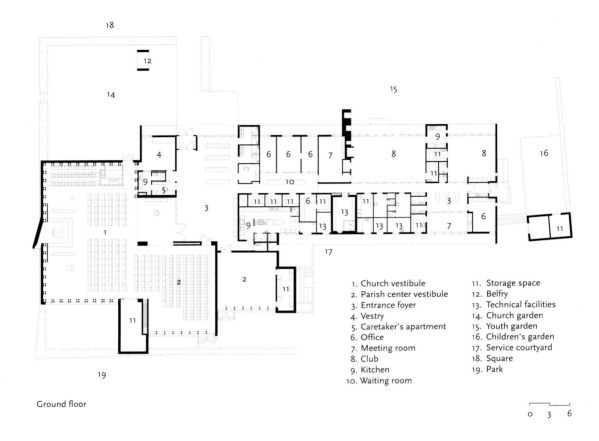

18

12

14

15

16

4

9

9

5

6 6 6 7 8 11 8

3 11

10

11 11 11 6 11 11 3

9 13 13 6

1 13 13 13 13 11 7

2 2 11

11

17

1. Church vestibule
2. Parish center vestibule
3. Entrance foyer
4. Vestry
5. Caretaker's apartment
6. Office
7. Meeting room
8. Club
9. Kitchen
10. Waiting room

11. Storage space
12. Belfry
13. Technical facilities
14. Church garden
15. Youth garden
16. Children's garden
17. Service courtyard
18. Square
19. Park

19

Ground floor

0   3   6

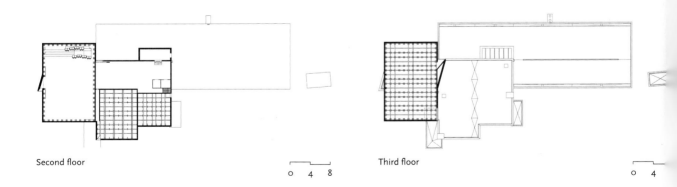

Second floor

0   4   8

Third floor

0   4

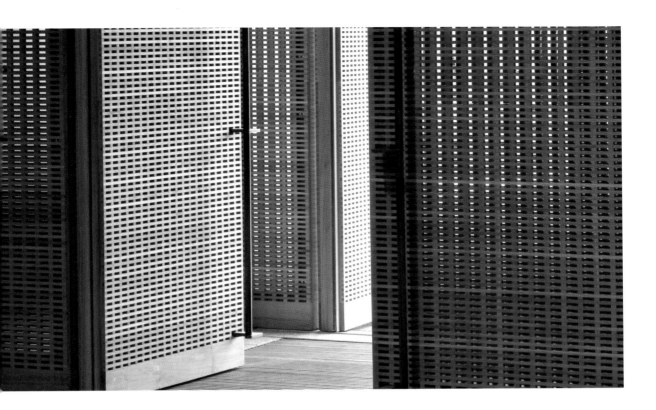

EVANGELICAL PARISH CENTER

Netzwerk Architekten | Mannheim, Germany | 2007

Religion: Evangelical Church

The design of this parish center, located in the district of Neuhermsheim, arose from a public tender that attracted more than 440 projects. The architects imagined a U-shaped space but with a quadrangular outline, a green roof and an oval-shaped garden in the middle.

The most important spaces are the vestibule, the group rooms and a covered outdoors area, as well as the main hall. With this distribution, the building affords parishioners different ambiances covering internal and semi-enclosed external spaces for holding events year-round. The garden leads outdoors in the northern section and becomes the heart of this meeting place. The architects designed two types of facades: the interior elevation is a long glass wall that can be opened up by sections. This makes it possible to see the garden from inside and unites the two spaces.

The exterior facade is an original structure of delicately perforated concrete pieces which stylizes the single-story construction. This facade delimits the interior without fully enclosing it, an expression of the parish opening up to its congregation and the community. The flexibility of the interior spaces is clear from the room configuration, as they can be distributed in different ways because of separating walls that permit multiple combinations: it is easier to communicate the vestibule and main room with the garden. Also, two tracks run around the main room and vestibule, and translucent curtains modify the size and feel of the rooms, affording greater privacy when called for.

^ Two rows of trees on the west and north sides will create a shady area between the building and the area of level ground. They also protect the parish center's garden.

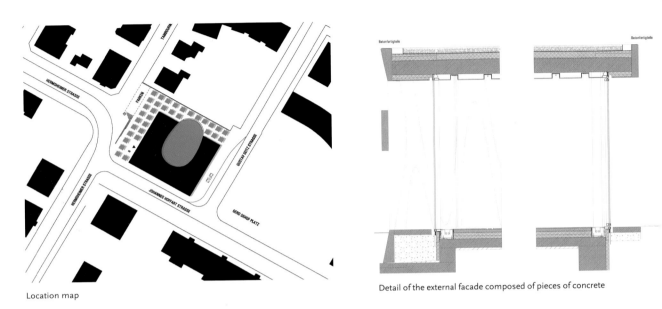

Location map

Detail of the external facade composed of pieces of concrete

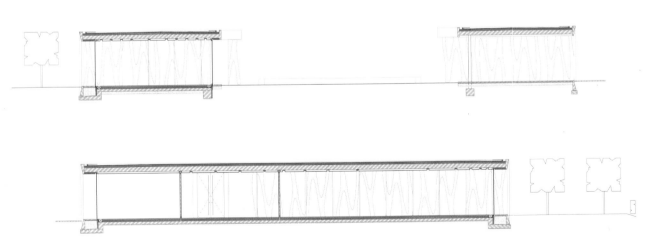

Sections

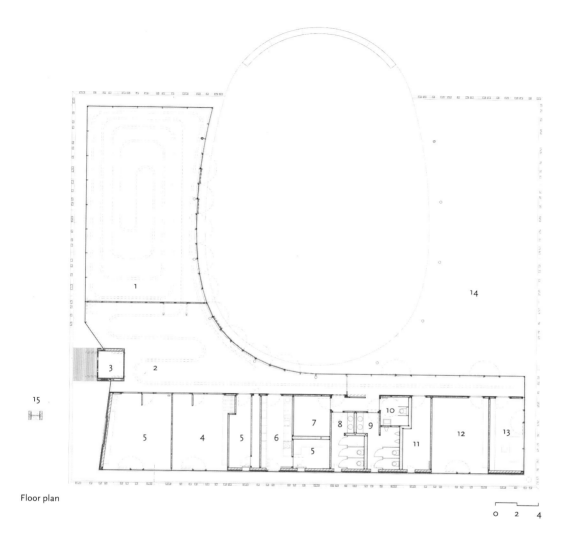

Floor plan

1. Main room
2. Lobby
3. Foyer
4. Group room
5. Closet
6. Kitchen
7. Technical equipment room
8. Ladies' toilet
9. Gentlemen's toilet
10. Disabled toilet
11. Storeroom
12. Youth room
13. Office
14. Covered outdoors area
15. Belfry

∧   The location of the building, connected with the outside via a passageway, situates the parish center in a large public area.

The interior glass facade permits a visual and physical connection with the outdoors and creates a relaxed and glowing ambiance.

HOUSE OF MEDITATION

Pascal Arquitectos | Bosques de las Lomas, Mexico City, Mexico | 2006
© Víctor Benítez

This building, used for wakes and as a religious space, encourages introspection and peace through the discreet use of materials and lighting. The architects were inspired by the architecture of the mastabas of ancient Egypt, i.e., funeral buildings made from sun-dried brick or stone, and the Mayan temples of Palenque. The rules to follow when building this type of space are very strict, so the architects sought advice and help from a group of rabbis.

The construction stands in a residential area and was designed to be completely isolated from the outside. To this end, an almost monolithic form was created that is very high and practically closed. The facades were covered in Grissal granite imported from Spain. Access to the inside of this house of meditation is via a triangular tunnel measuring 2m wide by 9m high. This solemn and austere space leads onto a large room lit by the sunlight that enters from the north through an interior courtyard. The courtyard includes a tall Dracaena marginata and a sculpture by the maestro Saul Kaminer, the only artwork in the building.

The simplicity and austerity of the space are the aspects that stand out the most. Inside, Camaru wood is used on the ceilings and in a simple pew which conceals the air-conditioning and lighting systems. The height of the room also acts as a decorative element and adds to the play of light and shadows formed by the skylight in the ceiling.

The combination of materials with pure, austere lines confers an aura of peace on the inside of the building.

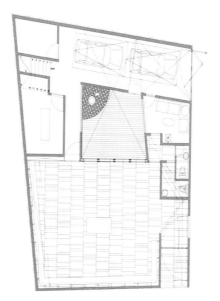

Ground floor

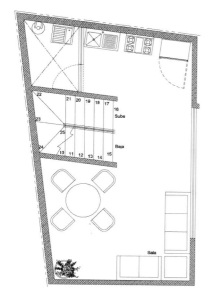

First floor

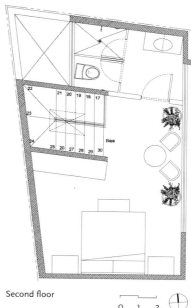

Second floor

The building includes a small apartment on the top floors for the caretaker.

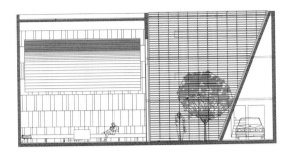

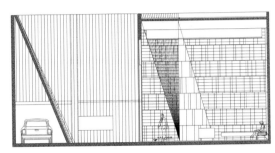

Longitudinal sections

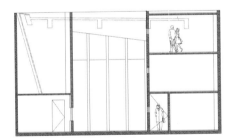

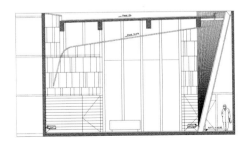

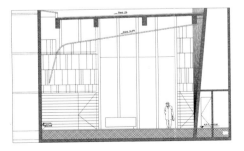

Cross-sections

^ Both the room and interior courtyard are sober spaces: the courtyard has been decorated with just one plant and a sculpture by Saúl Kaminer.

MOBILE CHAPEL

Hugo Dworzak | Mobile | 2007
© Harald Geiger

Religion: Catholic

The SC Austria Lustenau football team is famous for its post-match celebrations. Close by the grandstand are a number of wooden structures that form a small urban nucleus reminiscent of a market. Most are food stalls that make up an informal environment where some 4,000 people can celebrate the end of matches.

Club president Hubert Nagel decided to add a more spiritual aspect to the commercial environment created around the stadium because, in his words, "Every town has a church". As building regulations only permit easily dismountable structures, the wooden huts are all temporary. The small church was designed in line with these regulations but also to enable the structure to be moved around.

The church's measurements, i.e., 8.2 x 16.4 ft, are the same as a parking spot and its height allows it to pass under tunnels. Three of the chapel walls can open up to make it into an outdoor space which seen from above forms the shape of a cross. The interior was designed to feature horizontal floorboards with a slight gap between them. The exterior is covered with a translucent white membrane that accentuates the mobile nature of the structure. Natural lighting enters via the cracks in the boards to create a warm feeling inside, rendering windows unnecessary. Artificial lighting has been installed between the boards and the translucent membrane, lighting up both the interior and exterior of the chapel. The bell is the work of artist Udo Rabensteiner.

Although its usual location is outside the football stadium, it is not uncommon to see the church being driven through the streets of Lustenau to a wedding or baptism.

In this image we see the positioning of the artificial lighting. Because it is covered with a white membrane, the light is indistinct, creating a warmer ambiance.

Location

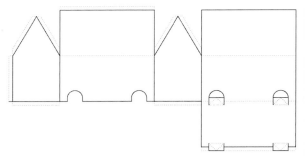

Model cutout

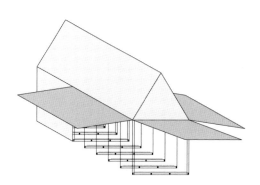

Axonometry of the structure

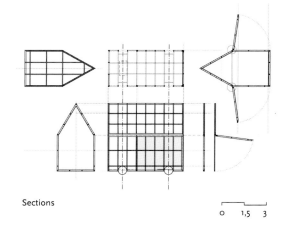

Sections

0   1,5   3

MOSQUE IN CHITTAGONG

Kasha Mahboob Chowdhury/Urbana | Chandgaon, Chittagong, Bangladesh | 2008

Religion: Islam

The design of a religious building, a mosque on this occasion, offers an architect the chance to examine and learn about the spiritual aspects and essences associated with each religion. Here the architect has sought to make the mosque not just a place of worship but also a space that permits meditation.

The semi-urban site affords great potential for making the mosque the cornerstone of the local community. The study began with identifying the essential elements of a mosque, such as the qiblah, mihrab and minbar. Building a mosque with a minimum of requisites made it possible to free up the other spaces from any traditional or cultural limitation and push the parameters of architectural design.

The space is formed of two identical square volumes. One acts as the courtyard in front of the mosque, i.e., the sahn, and the other is the mosque proper. The former has large openings which expose it to the elements. The circular opening in the roof is a reference to the spiritual, and the large side windows of the courtyard show the path surrounding the mosque. The latter stands out for its cupola, designed with a small opening protected by glass. This enables attendees to see the sky and permits the entry of light in the central spaces. Nighttime lighting ensures the mosque shines like a beacon and is another meeting place for the people. The design attempts to reflect the traditional nature of a mosque and at the same time add new uses to a typical place of prayer.

The mosque stands out against the landscape of rural Bangladesh and has become a new meeting place for the people.

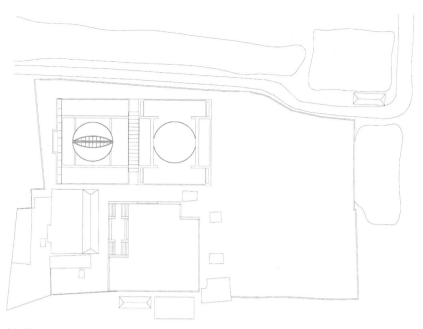

Location map

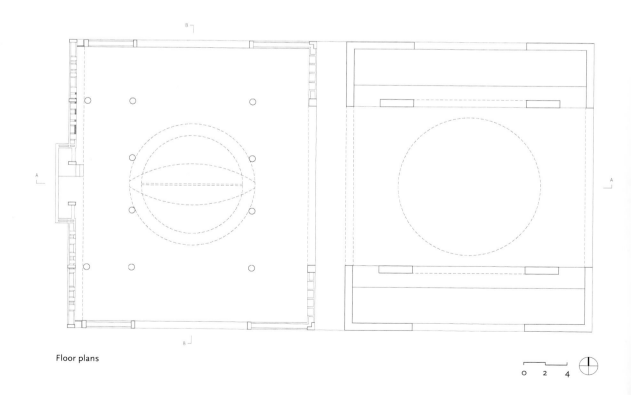

Floor plans

0 2 4

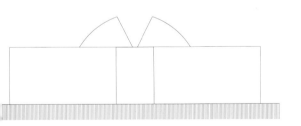

t elevation

South elevation

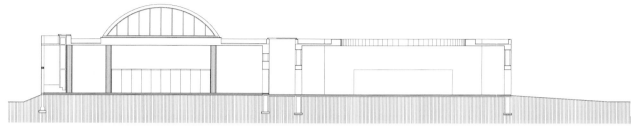

Longitudinal section

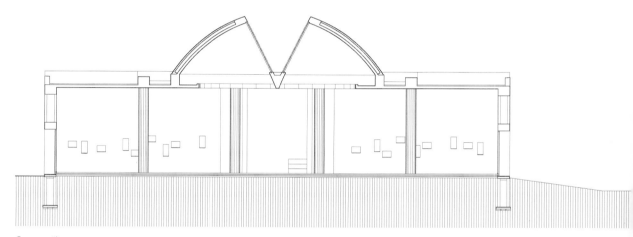

Cross-section

∧   The sections make it possible to observe the opening in the cupola of the mosque in detail, as well as the two new-build volumes.

PALACE OF PEACE AND RECONCILIATION

Foster & Partners | Astana, Kazakhstan | 2006

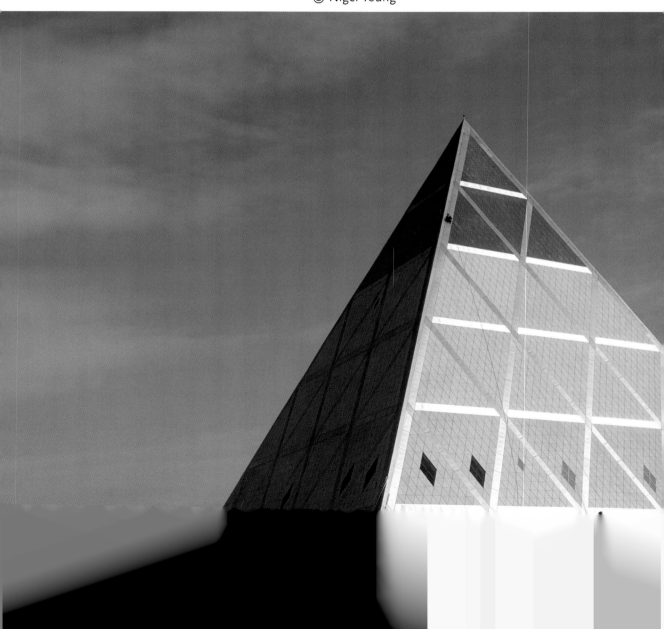

Religion: Multi-confessional

In September 2003, the Republic of Kazakhstan — the most extensive of the former Soviet republics — inaugurated the Congress of Leaders of World and Traditional Religions in the capital, Astana. The president of the Republic, encouraged by its success, decided to make it a triennial event. The Palace of Peace and Reconciliation was designed as the permanent seat of the Congress and a center for religious understanding, the renunciation of violence and equality amongst men. As well as representing the religious beliefs of the world, the Palace of Peace and Reconciliation houses an opera theater, educational facilities and a national center for the diversity of the ethnic groups of Kazakhstan. This diversity is unified within the symbol of a pyramid. The building is 203 ft tall and has a base that measures 203 x 203 ft. It is covered in stone with glass surfaces inserted in it. The space is organized around a raised central atrium. The assembly room, supported by four inclined pillars — the hands of peace — has been put at the top of the building. The architect used universal symbols for the design of the palace. The pyramid, with a spiritual history in Egypt, is a symbol of friendship for the future and a return to the main values common to the different religions: tolerance and the renunciation of violence. The colored glass is a metaphor for the transforming nature of art and symbolizes spiritual architecture. Blue and white represent peace, purity, humility and hope. The dove, a symbolic image in the Bible that Picasso popularized following World War II, is present as a universal symbol of peace.

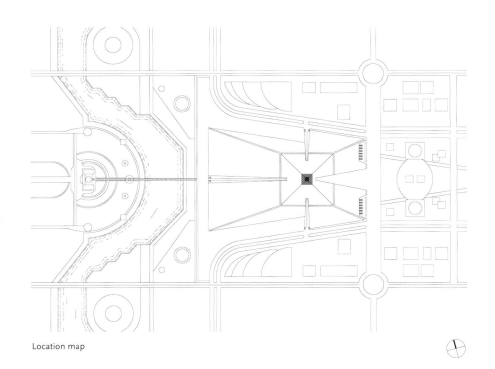

Location map

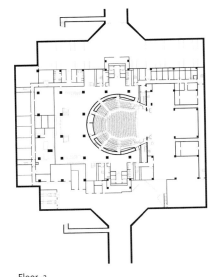

Floor -3

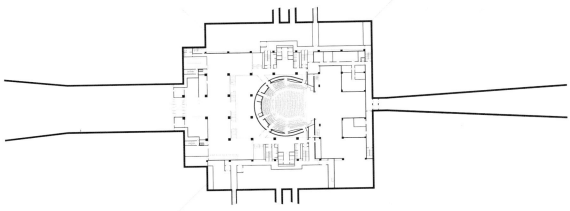

Floor -2

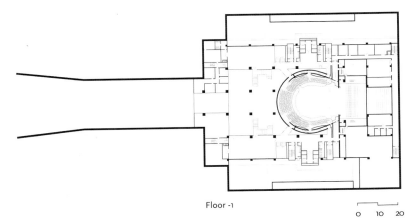

Floor -1

0   10   20

Ground floor

3rd floor

5th floor

6th floor

7th floor

8th floor

0   10   20

The strong oscillation of temperatures in this country and the short building time available led the architect to use pieces fabricated outside of Kazakhstan, which were assembled during the hottest months.

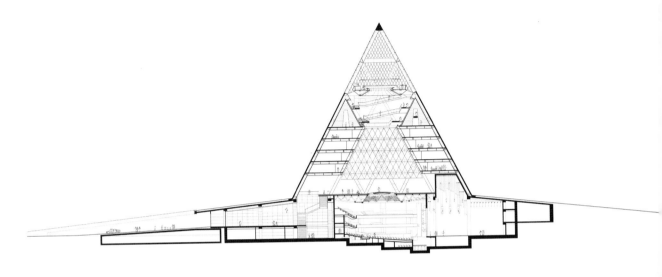

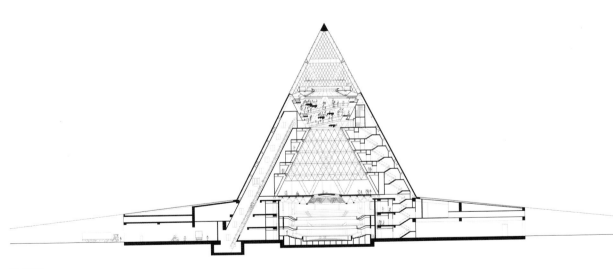

Sections

The construction also has an apex of colored glass, the work of Brian Clarke, located on the top vertex. The light penetrates through to the ground floor and the subterranean plants of the pyramid.

A lens in the atrium floor visually connects with the auditorium below. The light enters the room and generates a feeling of continuity between the highest and lowest points of the pyramid.

BAT YAHM TEMPLE

Lehrer Architects | Newport Beach, CA, USA | 1999

Religion: Judaism

According to the architects, Bat Yahm Temple is a spiritual campus with buildings and exterior spaces designed to create a place for the community, for dreaming of the divine and for transforming oneself with said dream. Sustainability and beauty become the rudiments of a spiritual and harmonious life.

The synagogue is located on the Pacific coast, in an area with a mild climate and lots of light. The design improvements have transformed the previous facility, a virtually windowless single building, into an ensemble of spaces that forms the new Torah Center. The sustainability elements included in the project involve control of daylight, natural ventilation, water management, permeable surfaces and native planting, among others.

The temple's parking lot is designed to meet two functions: to park vehicles and to act as a green area. The use of grass instead of traditional asphalt created a park (which is what the area is used for most of the time) which can, however, also be used for parking vehicles when necessary.

The image of Jacob's ladder, a symbol of the Jewish religion which symbolizes the union between Heaven and Earth, is represented here by a type of large skylight above the main nave. This skylight, mainly made out of glass, provides the building with natural lighting. The construction of this synagogue signifies the union of the kingdoms of Heaven and Earth. Light is the element that unites them, as, the rabbi says, spirit and light are synonymous.

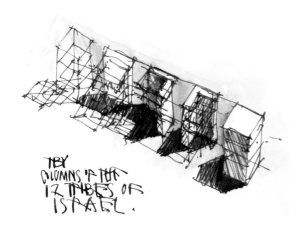

TRY
COLUMNS OF THE
12 TRIBES OF
ISRAEL.

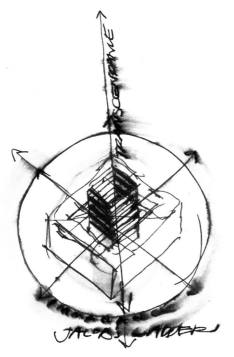

JACOBS LADDER

Sketches

Axonometry of the whole complex

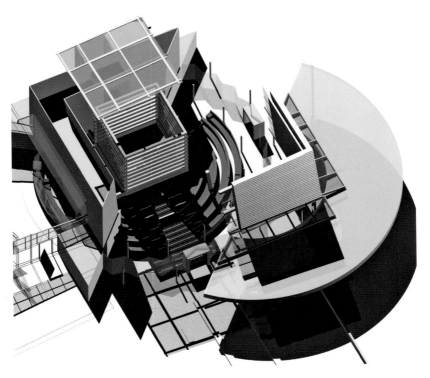

Axonometric view broken down into quarters

The parking lot is used as a park. The parking boundaries and zones are,delimited for when they are required.

The axonometric views show the volume of the synagogue and the buildings around it. Below is an exploded view of the round main room and the spectacular skylight that symbolizes Jacob's ladder.

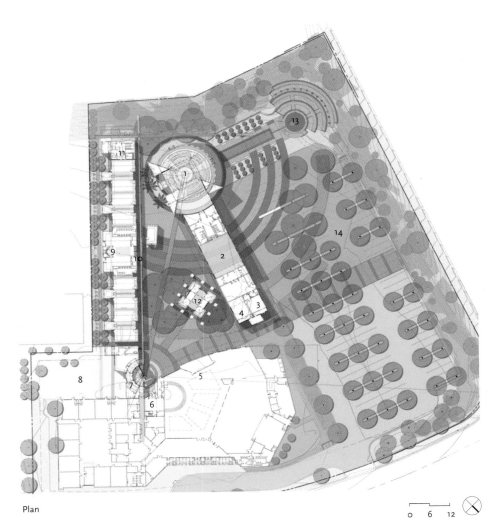

Plan

0   6   12

1. Chapel and tower of
   the Ark
2. Social Hall
3. Cantor's Studio
4. Board room
5. Existing Sanctuary
6. Rabbi's Perch
7. Campus Hub
8. Children's
   playground

9. Processional alley
10. Walkway of light
11. Mikvah courtyard
12. Library and courtyard
13. Sacred garden and
    amphitheatre
14. Parking park

CHURCH IN SEVESO

Gregotti Associati | Baruccana di Seveso, Italy | 2008
© Donato di Bello

Religion: Catholic

The Baruccana parish center is located on the outskirts of Seveso, in the Milan metropolitan area. It is formed of a number of sports fields and a building complex. The main volumes are the church, a multi-purpose room, a gym, an oratory and the apartments for the parish priest and coadjutor. A road ending in the large courtyard outside the church entrance is the principal nexus between the parish buildings and the center of town. The different volumes come together around this courtyard and its distribution gives it the look of a small town. The church has a modern design: the stone covering and the location of the bells — outside and with the mechanism exposed — complement its contemporary lines.

The church is a parallelepiped volume crowned by an oblong volume and a belfry. The main entrance and side doors stand out for the openings in the volume, which function as atriums. A space to the right of the main door has been designed to house the font. The inside of the church is divided into three parts: the first comprises the entrance, the confessional boxes, the stairs leading to a ladies' gallery and the font; the second is formed by the main nave which seats 500 people, while the third is made up of the winter chapel, vestry and auxiliary rooms.

The main nave is lit by the large oblong-shaped windows in the ceiling and practicable openings at ground level. The structure is of reinforced concrete, laid with wooden floorboards. The parish priest and coadjutant's rooms fan out around a courtyard reached by a covered vestibule.

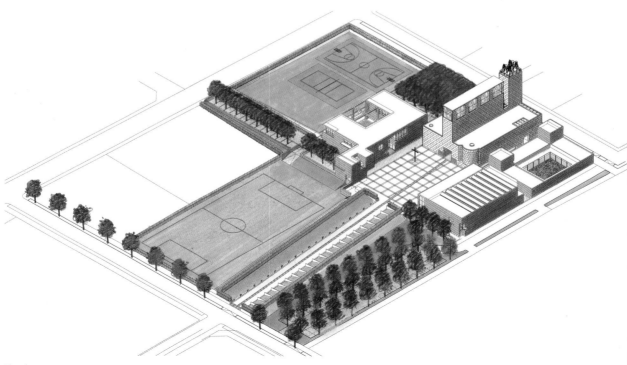

Sketches

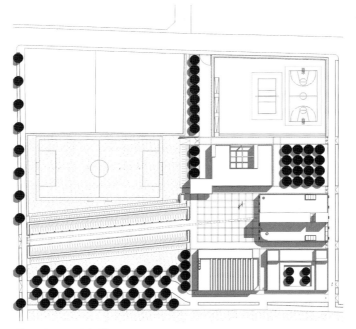

Floor plan, parish buildings

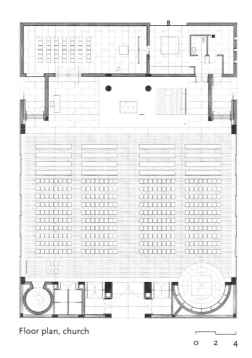

Floor plan, church

0   2   4

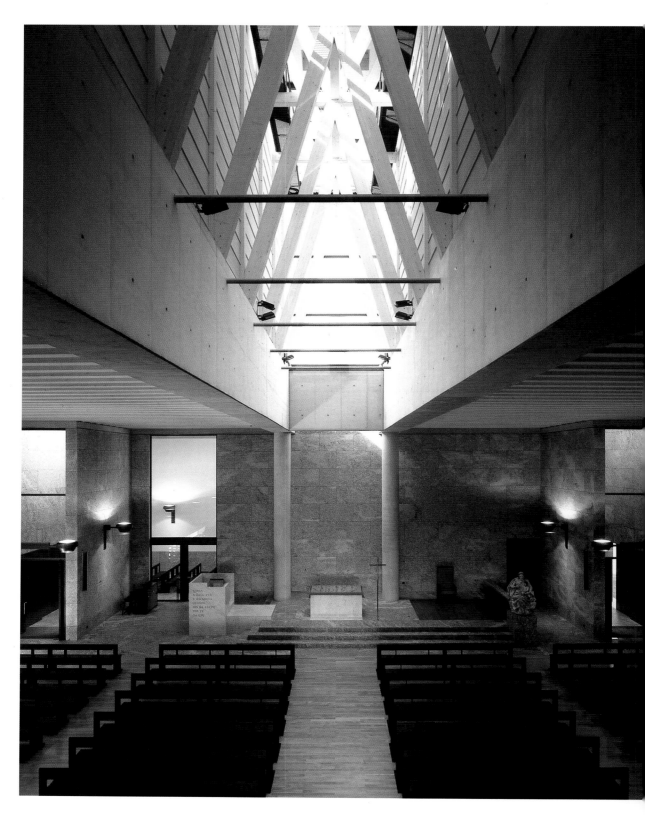

The oblong volume that crowns the main nave has openings to let the light in. A metal platform makes it possible to surround the wooden beams of the volume.

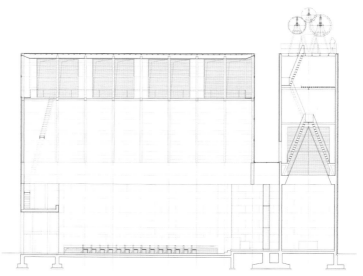

Longitudinal section

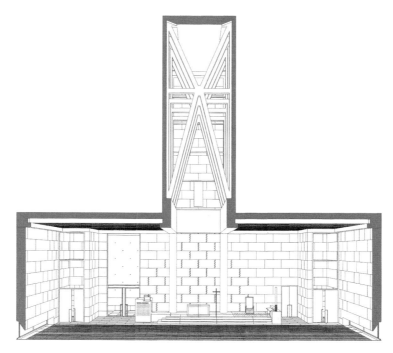

Cross-section in perspective

ISLAMIC FORUM

Jasarevic Architects | Penzberg, Germany | 2005
© Alen Jasarevic, Angelika Bardehle, Nursen Ozlukurt

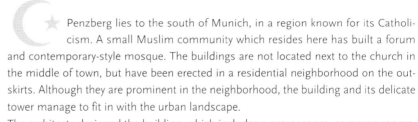

Penzberg lies to the south of Munich, in a region known for its Catholicism. A small Muslim community which resides here has built a forum and contemporary-style mosque. The buildings are not located next to the church in the middle of town, but have been erected in a residential neighborhood on the outskirts. Although they are prominent in the neighborhood, the building and its delicate tower manage to fit in with the urban landscape.

The architects designed the building, which includes a prayer room, common rooms, a library and an apartment, on an L-shaped floor plan. The facades, most covered in pale stone, indicate the functions of each room. The entrance boasts two concrete slabs simulating an open door to welcome people in Arabic and German. The main door, made from stainless steel, is open to everyone. Upon entering one sees a staircase and well-lit entrance hall. The view to the right is of a lovely prayer room. Daylight penetrates from one side via the curved concrete slabs. The blue glass wall illuminates the qiblah, i.e., the element that faces Mecca. This project is the work of the artists Lutzenberger & Lutzenberger, from Bad Wörishofen, along with Mohammed Mandi from Abu Dhabi. The other rooms function as in any parish center and are the setting for German classes or prayers. The project takes in Muslim culture, religion and mindset and applies them to the development of contemporary religious architecture. Here, modern architecture is helping in the gradual integration of the different beliefs that are deep-seated amongst the population.

Im Namen Gottes,
des Allerbarmers,
des Barmherzigen.
Lob sei Gott dem Herrn
der Welten.
Dem Allerbarmer,
dem Barmherzigen.
Dem Herrscher am Tage
des Gerichtes.
Dir dienen wir und Dich
bitten wir um Hilfe
Führe uns auf den rechten
Weg, den Weg derer,
denen Du gnädig bist,
nicht derer, denen Du
zürnst und nicht der
Irregehenden.
Im Namen Gottes,
des Allerbarmers,
des Barmherzigen.
Ihr Menschen!
Wir haben euch aus
Mann und Frau erschaffen
und haben euch zu
Völkern und Stämmen
werden lassen, damit ihr
euch kennenlernt.
Der Edelste vor Gott ist
der Gerechteste
unter euch
Gott hat das wahre
Wort gesprochen.

Although prominent in the neighborhood, the building and its delicate tower manage to fit into the urban landscape, as the urban structure and traditional architecture had already been modified through different buildings made in styles that fall between rustic and monotonous postwar designs.

The qiblah, which indicates the direction of Mecca, stands out for the bright blue light that illuminates it.

Both the mihrab, the small niche Muslims face when praying, and the minbar, i.e., the pulpit in the form of a staircase from which the imam delivers his sermons, are elements that link the Islamic tradition with a contemporary aesthetic.

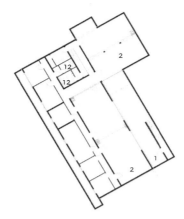

Basement

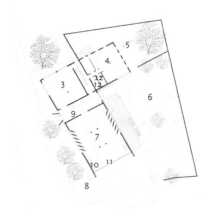

Ground floor

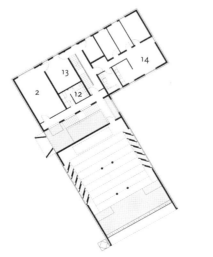

First floor

1. Courtyard
2. Multipurpose space
3. Library
4. Room for special purposes
5. Garden
6. Parking lot
7. Mosque
8. Minaret
9. Vestibule
10. Minbar
11. Mihrab
12. Rest rooms
13. Office
14. Living quarters

0   3   6

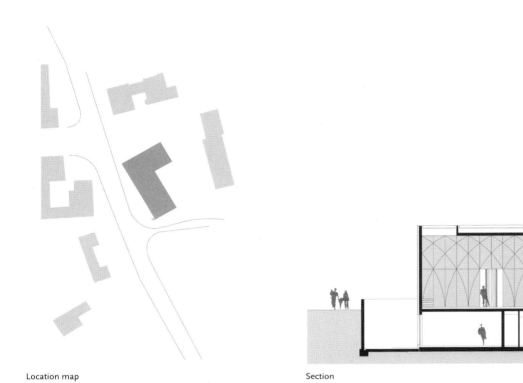

Location map

Section

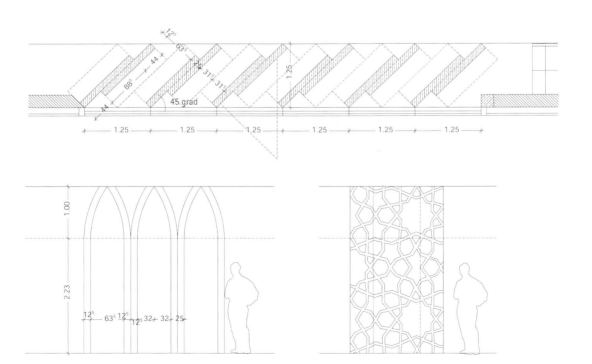

Details of different architectural and decorative elements

Geometry is very important in Islamic tradition. One highlight of this mosque is the decoration of the mihrab, a composition of stars containing the 99 names of God.

SYNAGOGUE IN DRESDEN

Wandel Hoefer Lorch & Hirsch | Dresden, Germany | 2002
© Norbert Miguletz

Religion: Judaism

Architecture in the city of Dresden is related to two historic facts: the destruction of the Gottfried Semper synagogue during Kristallnacht on 9 November 1938 and the bombing of the historical center in February 1945 by the Allied forces. The reconstruction of the city reproduced the historical monuments and established a false continuity and aspiration of architectural stability. Architects Wandel Hoefer Lorch & Hirsch, however, took building a synagogue as a challenge, an example of the conflict between fragility and stability, the permanent and the temporary. Set on a sloping plot, the new construction has a courtyard which acts as an element of connection between the synagogue and the community center. Coherence is maintained by the use of the same material in both buildings, i.e., fine sheets of pre-cut stone. The design of the synagogue, a space for prayer and meditation, explores the differences between materials: the almost monolithic structure of the exterior contrasts with the textile and metallic materials used inside.

The synagogue's structure also slowly turns, following the geometry of the site and the requirement to face east. Inside, of note is an elegant metal fabric suspended from the square concrete ceiling and surrounding the prayer area. This fabric, developed by a clothing manufacturer, provides a special light with the reflections it creates. The wooden furniture indoors is characterized by its different sizes. The pews, lectern and niche with the Torah on the eastern wall stand out.

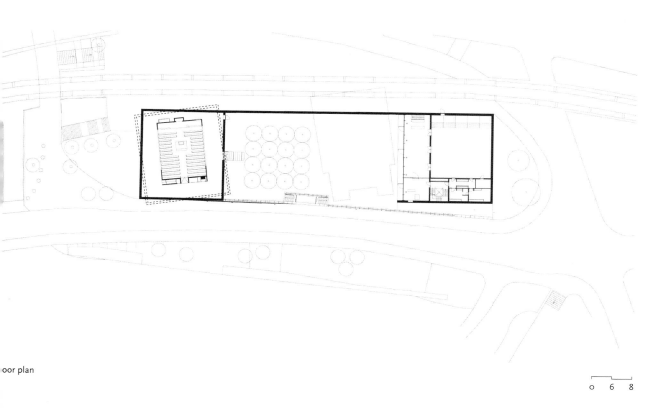

oor plan

0   6   8

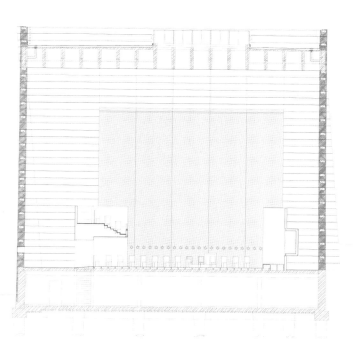

Section

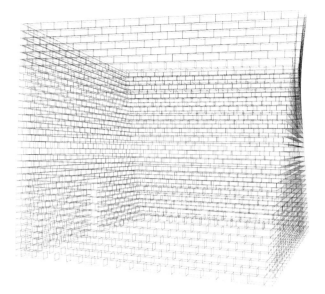

Perspective showing how the synagogue structure turns

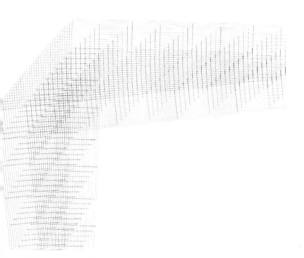

Detail of the intersection of the stone blocks

Detail of one corner of the structure

This complex volume is composed of 41 orthogonal layers formed of 120 x 60 x 60 cm stone blocks that turn gradually until the desired orientation is reached.

^ Jewish symbols such as the Star of David and the Menorah stand out against the simplicity of the interior design.

SANTO VOLTO CHURCH

Mario Botta | Turin, Italy | 2006
© Enrico Cano

Religion: Catholic

As in many European cities, the urban fabric of Turin has undergone a number of changes in recent decades. Extensive underutilized industrial areas are being transformed into new post-industrial economic realities. In this context of change, the Archbishop of Turin, His Eminence Cardinal Severino Poletto, decided to build a liturgical and community center on Via Borgaro, a street previously occupied by a steelworks.

The project provided for the construction of a church dedicated to the Holy Shroud. It has a heptagonal floor plan surrounded by seven towers connected to chapels. The truncation at the top of the towers and chapels created a number of openings that function as skylights. The heptagonal floor plan, of strong symbolic and religious significance, sees the main axis face toward the city.

The new parish center brings together all the previously dispersed services. Beneath the main nave is a conference room. Other areas include offices, apartments, a chapel for daily services and living quarters for the parish priest. The design of the new center included an old chimney, testament to the area's industrial past. It also required the architect designing a reference to the Holy Shroud to put behind the altar. To that end, he used a binary image comprising black and white pixels to recreate the face on the Shroud. These pixels were made with small red marble bricks from Verona, positioned so that the face of Christ would appear when the light fell on them.

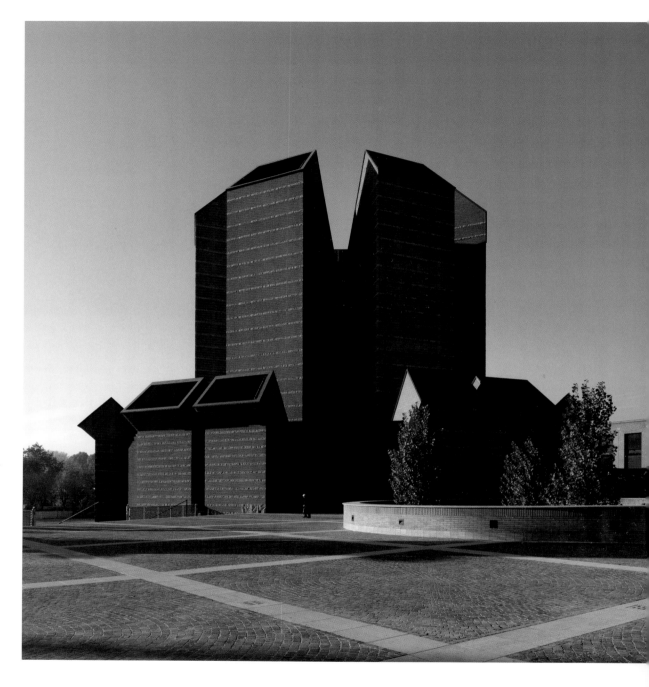

∧   The monumental appearance of the outside of the new church contrasts with the inside of the main nave, which is very warm despite its large size.

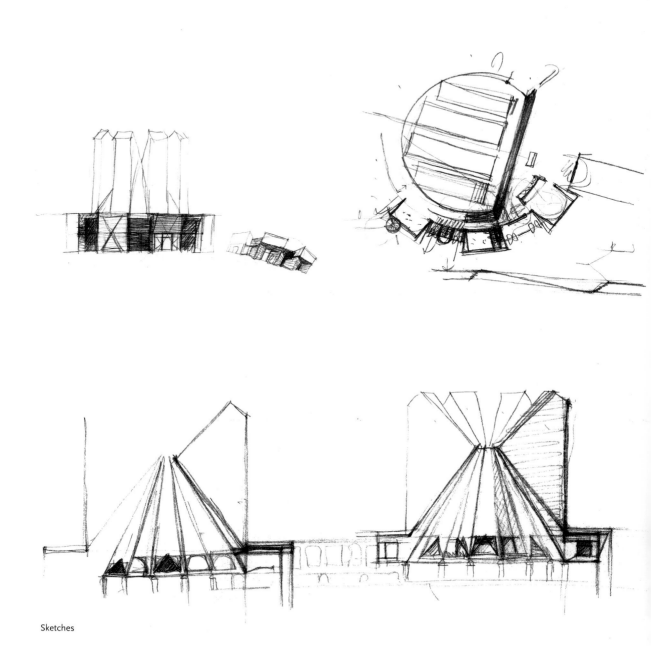

Sketches

Natural light enters the church thanks to the skylights created by truncating the towers and chapels.

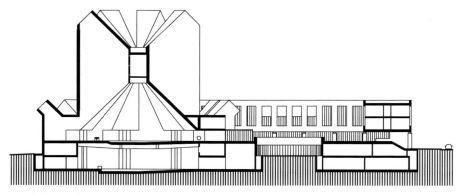

Longitudinal section

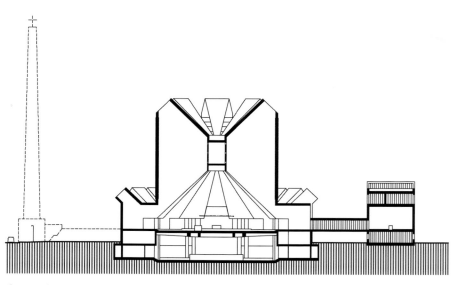

Cross-section

∧ The towers are located around a cylinder suspended above the main nave. The base of the chapel is connected with the base of the towers.

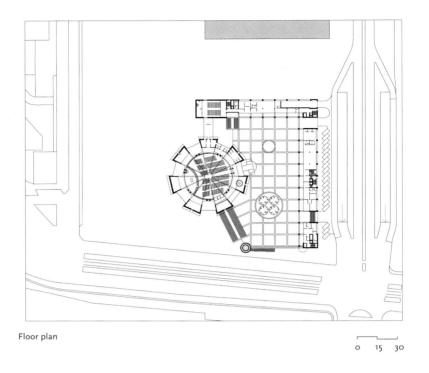

Floor plan

SAINT FRANÇOIS DE MOLITOR CHURCH

Corinne Callies, Jean-Marie Duthilleul/AREP | Paris, France | 2005
© Pep Escoda

Religion: Catholic

This new church in rue Molitor is the reconstruction of the old parish church from 1941. The small size and lack of safety of the building materials in the original church tipped the balance in favor of a practically new building. The Bible and the life of St. Francis of Assisi — to whom the church is dedicated — are evoked to establish the relations between a city (Jerusalem) and an outdoor garden (the image of Eden). The building is a large volume formed of marble and translucent glass panels which make it possible to illuminate the rooms. From the outside, nothing indicates its religious function except for three large doors that give way to the portico and belfry. These are crossed to reach the narthex, a silent, dimly lit space that permits a transition from the hustle and bustle outside to the spiritual silence inside the nave. Of note here is the arrangement of the pews around an altar in the center. The font is right at the entrance, but the most surprising element is the garden behind the glass wall at the back, which aims to represent nature in its pure state, i.e., the place where St. Francis blessed all creatures. In front of the cross near the translucent wall is the ambo, a lectern from which the Scriptures are read. Two curved walls divide the space, supporting a number of galleries and delimiting spaces such as the storeroom, vestry and a small tabernacle. The ceiling is a horizontal structure in the form of boxes that let in the light that illuminates the altar.

∧   The architects have managed to create a space impregnated with calm thanks to the materials used (stone, wood and glass) and a timeless design. The altar, sunk into the floor of the nave, represents a reference to the Bible.

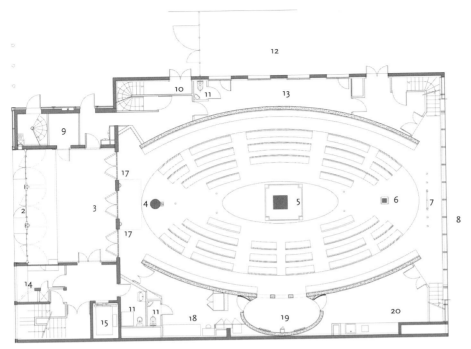

Ground floor

1. Rue Molitor
2. Porch
3. Narthex
4. Font
5. Altar
6. Ambo
7. Cross
8. Garden
9. Meeting room
10. Parking lot exit
11. Rest room
12. Passage
13. Storeroom
14. Reception
15. Elevator
16. Gallery
17. Fonts
18. Vestry
19. Tabernacle
20. Flower storage room

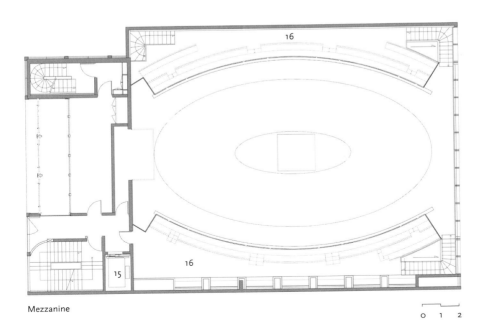

Mezzanine

0   1   2

The main entry of light is the large glass wall on the south axis of the church. Through it one can see the Japanese arches and the grass that grows in the garden.

FUENTE NUEVA CHAPEL

F3 Architects | Rupanco, Chile | 2006
© Ignacio Infante

Religion: Catholic

✝ This small private chapel is located next to Rupanco Lake which covers 23,000 hectares in the province of Osorno, southern Chile. The chapel responded to one main objective: to build a place that would enable the development of the Catholic liturgy, as well as being a space for reflection and retreat. The land on which it is built has a pronounced slope, although a small landing affords incredible views across the lake. The architects designed a chapel measuring just 226 sq ft with a capacity limited to 12 people. The small building gains volume thanks to a wooden terrace running from the entrance and forming a platform used for outdoor ceremonies. The simplicity of the design and the materials chosen for the construction are part of a deliberately sought-after austerity.

The materials, i.e., wood and glass, are simply applied, easy to find close to the site and very low-cost compared with other building materials. The impregnated pine wood manages to give a unitary aspect to the chapel, and the outdoor and inside walls, ceiling and floor merge in a single volume. The east facade, where the altar is, includes a glass wall that enables parishioners to look directly out over the lake and mountains. In this fantastic natural setting, the Fuente Nueva Chapel manages to convey peace and harmony and a feeling of religiousness that transcends any belief.

Church elements, such as the cross, belfry, etc., have been simplified to achieve a unique volume where no one thing stands out above anything else. The entrance is beneath a small porch which follows the form of the roof.

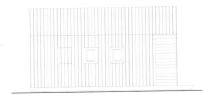

North elevation

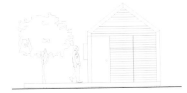

West elevation

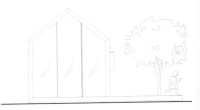

East elevation

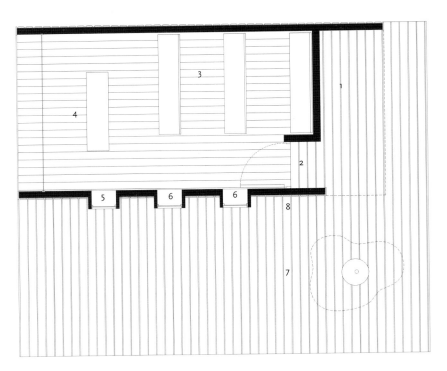

Floor plan

1. Porch
2. Entrance
3. Nave
4. Altar
5. Sacrarium
6. Niche
7. Terrace
8. Belfry

0   0,5   1

A natural setting is the ideal backdrop for the building. The church sits on sharply sloping land and the surface was cut to create a flat space for the chapel, from where the views can be appreciated.

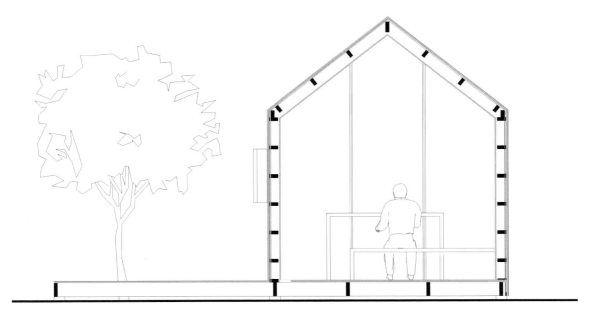

Section

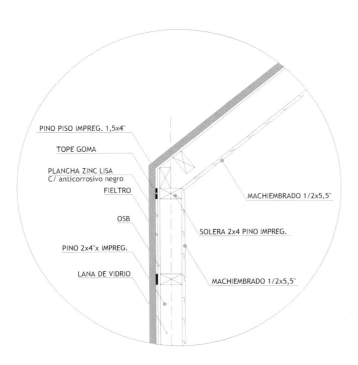

PINO PISO IMPREG. 1,5x4"

TOPE GOMA

PLANCHA ZINC LISA
C/ anticorrosivo negro

FIELTRO

OSB

PINO 2x4"x IMPREG.

LANA DE VIDRIO

MACHIEMBRADO 1/2x5,5"

SOLERA 2x4 PINO IMPREG.

MACHIEMBRADO 1/2x5,5"

Detail of the roof construction

RAMAT SHALOM MIKVEH

Pascal Arquitectos | Lomas de Tecamachalco, Mexico | 2006
© Víctor Benítez

Religion: Judaism

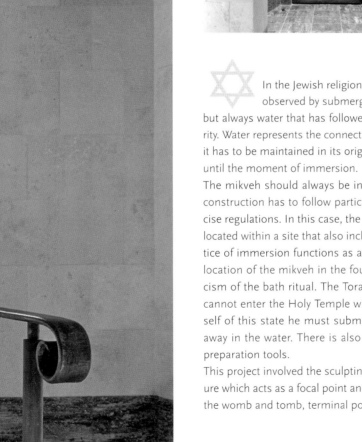

In the Jewish religion, the mikveh is a ritual purification bath. The ritual is observed by submerging oneself in water either from a spring or the rain, but always water that has followed a number of strict procedures related with its purity. Water represents the connection between humankind and the Garden of Eden, so it has to be maintained in its original state and neither man nor woman may touch it until the moment of immersion.

The mikveh should always be in contact with the floor, i.e., with the earth, and its construction has to follow particular measurements and materials, adjusted to precise regulations. In this case, the requirements were hard to achieve as the mikveh is located within a site that also includes a synagogue and community center. The practice of immersion functions as an act of renewal and rebirth. For the architects, the location of the mikveh in the foundations of the building is related with the mysticism of the bath ritual. The Torah holds that when a man is in an impure state he cannot enter the Holy Temple without suffering severe punishment. To divest himself of this state he must submerge himself in the mikveh, so his sins may wash away in the water. There is also a mikveh to purify kitchen instruments and food-preparation tools.

This project involved the sculpting of solid marble and the result is an impressive figure which acts as a focal point and sculptural element. The mikveh is also related with the womb and tomb, terminal points in the cycle of life.

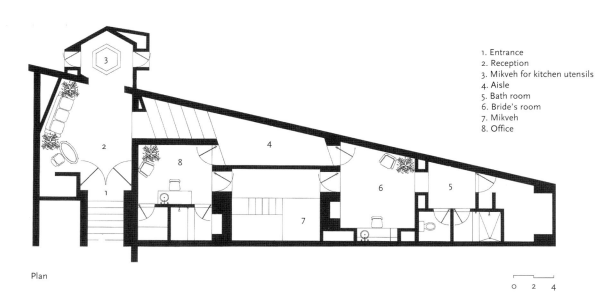

1. Entrance
2. Reception
3. Mikveh for kitchen utensils
4. Aisle
5. Bath room
6. Bride's room
7. Mikveh
8. Office

Plan

0   2   4

ONO KYOTO ZEN LOUNGE

Waro Kishi & K Associates Architects | Kyoto, Japan | 2003
© Hiroyuki Hirai

Religion: Buddhism

Ono Kyoto is an urban temple designed for the members of the Buddhist sect Zen Soto. Although one of its goals was to sell Buddhist items, clothing and altar objects, it is mainly used for conversations between Buddhist priests, who are the people that really frequent the space.

Despite a small store window that can be seen from the street, the temple was designed not to be recognized as a store. The surfaces largely define the nature of the temple. There are horizontal ones such as the floating parquet wood and tables for which the architect chose the materials with great care, being surfaces people have direct contact with. He used unusual finishes such as Japanese chestnut and Zelkova wood.

Also of interest are three vertical surfaces. The first is a floating steel screen in a rusty black color, 6 mm thick and located inside a glass sheet to make it transparent and emery-polished. This glass and metal panel prevents people from seeing out and only permits light to enter. The second surface is a dark brick wall in the middle of the space. The third and final surface is an L-shaped piece of fabric.

The vertical and horizontal surfaces define this religious space — called Dogen for the name of the founder of the Soto sect — and make the atmosphere so special. The idea was to create a retreat in the middle of town and a space where it would be possible to psychologically cut oneself off from the bustle of the city.

^ The materials stand out for their simplicity. Wood, sheets of glass and steel, and bricks. The robust brick wall, soft fabric and stability of the gla and metal sheets generate a harmonious and balanced space.

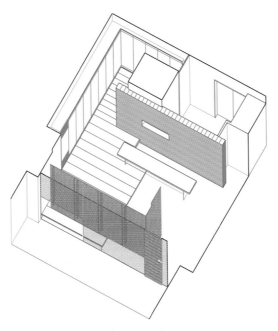

Axonometry

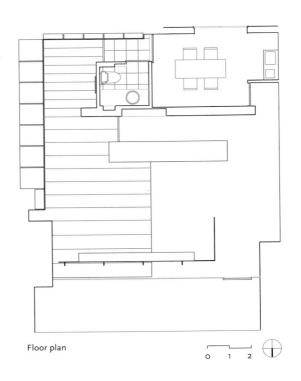

Floor plan

0   1   2

For the architect, the design of this building resembled that of a hall or a chapel more than a business.

∧   The dark colors and minimalist lines create spaces that exude spirituality.

NEW CEMETERY IN CASTELLÓN

Emilio Llobat Guarino | Castellón de la Plana, Spain | 2007
© Emilio Llobat

Religion: Multi-confessional

This new religious building forms part of a complex that offers funeral services for the population of a town two kilometers away. The complex includes funeral homes, offices, a crematory oven, a room for religious ceremonies and various courtyards. There is a sense of spirituality in the air, particularly because of the simplicity of the lines and the intelligent way light is treated — the site is positioned to ensure the natural lighting changes over the course of the day and the spaces are perceived differently.

With this new ensemble of buildings, people can take leave of their loved ones in a setting of peace and serenity. Particular religious references have been avoided as it is a multi-confessional place where all religions are welcomed, and there is also the possibility of making no reference to any belief or particular type of worship. Entrance to the spiritual place is via a southwest-facing courtyard which acts as a transition space between the street and the calm of the interior.

White, symbolizing purity and simplicity, is present inside and out. Baseboards created with treated rusty iron sheets have a double function: they protect the walls and symbolize the Earth. Of note are two interior courtyards of Oriental inspiration located next to the funeral homes and crematorium, designed for meditation and with a heavy spiritual weight. The materials used are stone with beech crossbeams for the floor, wooden pews, white gravel and bamboo.

The high walls of the entrance courtyard are not completely closed. This creates an interesting play of light and shadows that change over the course of the day.

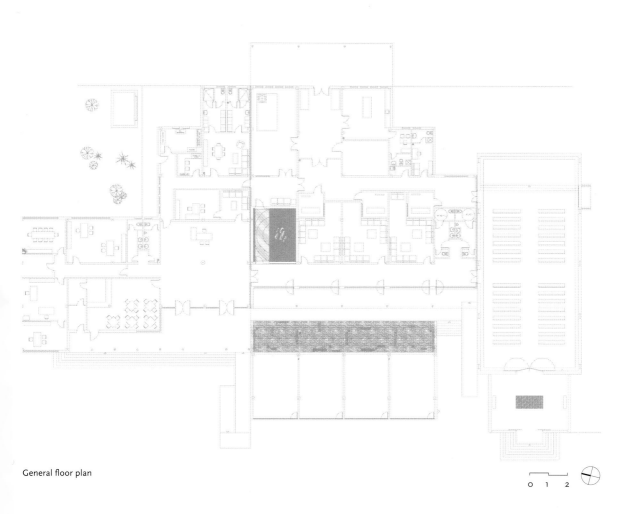

General floor plan

0 1 2

The white color chosen for the building symbolizes purity and simplicity, and the rusty color of the iron sheets represents the Earth. The two combine to create a contrast which represents the spiritual and the earthly.

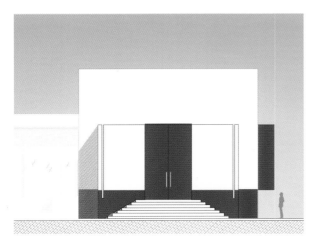

South elevation

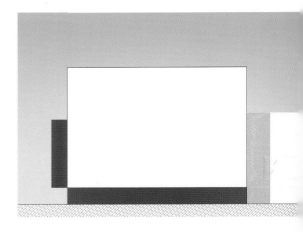

East elevation

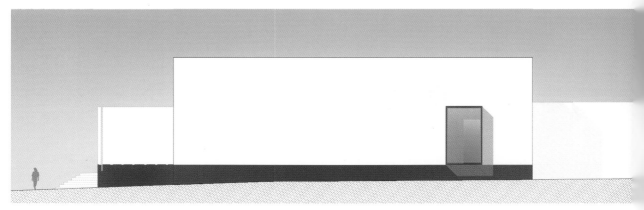

West elevation

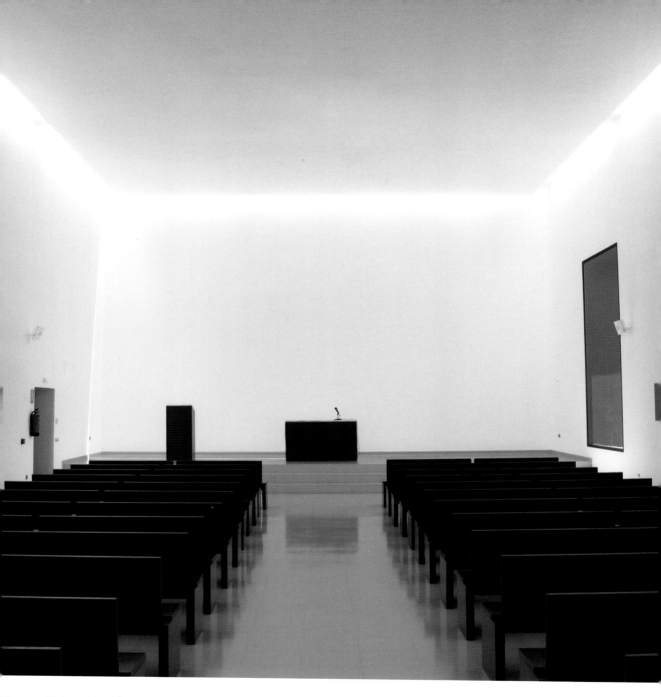

The play of light and shadows is also present inside the building. The suspended ceiling and a large window favor the changing natural lighting.

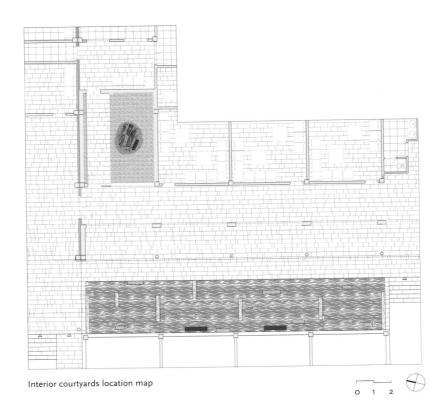

Interior courtyards location map

0 1 2

Floor plan in front of the crematorium

0 0.5 1

Floor plan of the courtyard in front of the funeral homes

Diagram of the layout of the courtyard elements

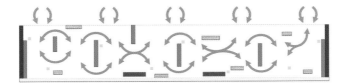

Diagram of courtyard circulation

ST. HENRY'S ECUMENICAL ART CHAPEL

Matti Sanaksenaho & Pirjo Sanaksenaho/Sanaksenaho Architects | Turku, Finland | 2005
© Jussi Tiainen

This chapel stands on a hill near Turku, a town on the Finnish island of Hirvensalo, and is surrounded by a series of oncology services buildings. The shape of the complex, both outside and in, represents a fish with enormous copper scales. The fish is a symbol from the early years of Christianity and here emerges from a hill surrounded by trees. The copper surface of the chapel will become green over time and bring the building into harmony with the color of the surrounding trees. Access inside is via a ramp that connects with the main vestibule. A passageway which includes the toilets and a number of auxiliary rooms leads to the large main nave, the stomach of the fish. The chapel was built not just as a place of worship but also to house art exhibitions; the pews at the end of the nave can be removed to increase the exhibition space. Inside, the use of wood typical to Nordic countries prevails. Laminated and pasted pine wood ribs have been used along with waxed wooden floorboards and solid alder pews.

The lighting is another of the most carefully considered aspects in the design of this religious space: the translucent altar windows, the work of artist Hannu Konola, are at the top of the church, and a skylight in the vestibule lights up the entrance zone. The interior wood is lit with small points of artificial light. The design of the church, the location of the entries of natural light and the texture of the wood produce an attractive contrast between light and shadows.

The architects wanted to give a sculptural shape to the construction and opted for a design in the shape of a fish, a symbol of Christianity. The copper surface will turn green over time and bring the building into harmony with the color of the surrounding trees.

Sketches

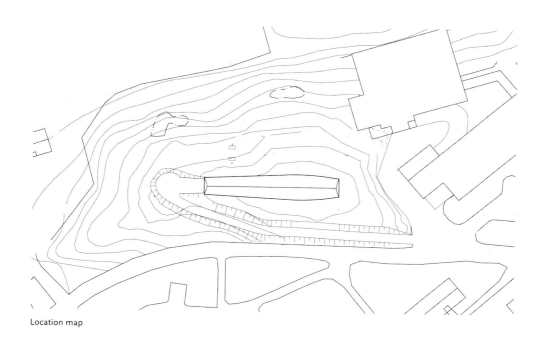

Location map

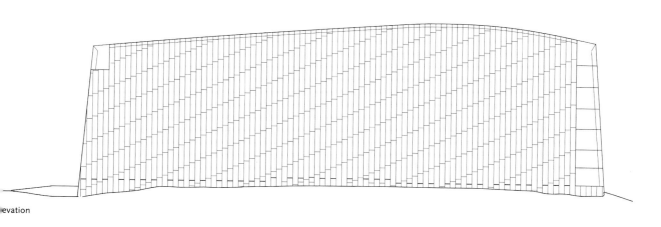

Elevation

The sketches show the simplicity of the architects' idea: a compact and majestic structure that stands on a hill.

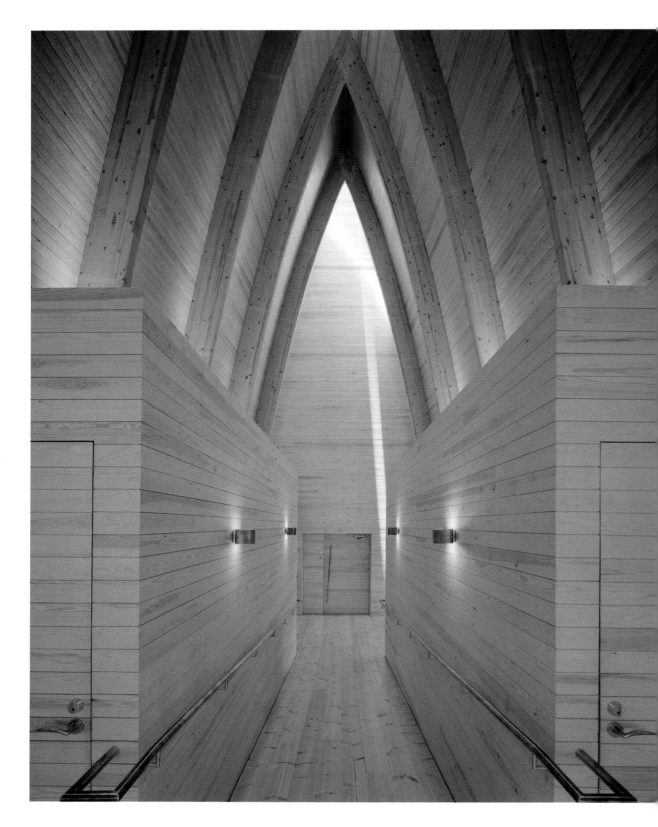

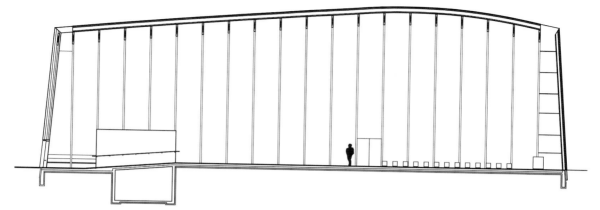

Longitudinal section

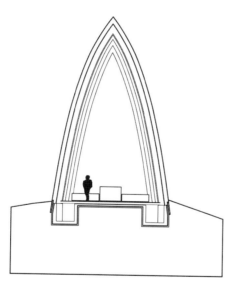

Cross-section

The copper used on the exterior casing and the wood featured indoors are the main materials used in this church. The wood creates a warm and cozy atmosphere, perfect for welcoming the faithful.

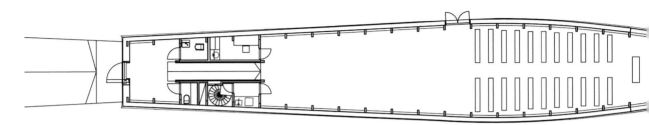

Floor plan

0   2

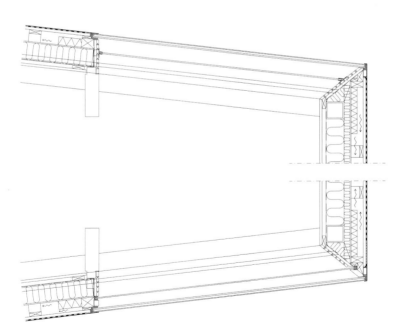

Detail of the altar windows

LEAF CHAPEL

Klein Dytham Architecture | Yamanashi, Japan | 2004
© Katsuhisa Kida

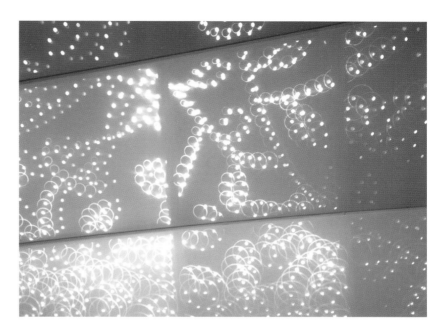

Religion: Christian

This small chapel is located on the grounds of a hotel in Kobuchizawa, in a green area with a pond and magnificent views across Mount Fuji and the Yatsugatake peaks, the Japanese Alps. The chapel, dedicated almost exclusively to wedding ceremonies, is formed of two large leaves, one of steel and the other of glass, which have seemingly fluttered to the ground. The glass leaf with its delicate lace pattern motif emulates a pergola and the structure holding it up reminds one of the veins of a leaf which slowly become thinner the further they get from the central stem.

The white steel leaf, perforated with 4,700 holes, each of which hold an acrylic lens, is similar to bride's veil made of delicate lace. Light filters through the lenses and projects a lace pattern onto the white fabric inside. As the day goes on, the light changes and transforms the pattern of the perforated structure, which changes into a myriad of shapes and motifs that frame the wedding ceremony. At the end of the ceremony when the groom lifts the bride's veil, the 'steel veil' magically opens too, revealing the pond and the enchanting nature beyond. Although it lifts 11 tons, the mechanism raises the structure silently and in just 38 seconds.

Dark elements inside the chapel emphasize the whiteness of the structure. The floor is made from black granite and some walls have been covered in darkened wood. The wooden pews, also black, are complemented with transparent acrylic backs with motifs encapsulated on them that represent light green flowers. The Chinese writing on these flowers, *rempukusou*, means 'good luck'.

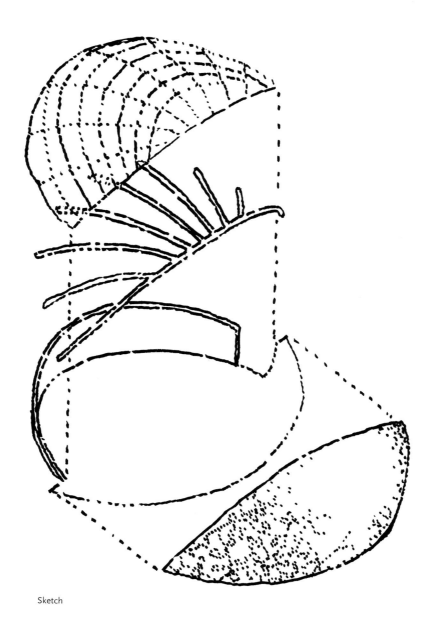

Sketch

This simple illustration shows the exploded view of the structures that form the two leaves of the chapel.

∧   When the ceremony ends, guests walk over stopping stones across the pond. When a ceremony is held at night, the chapel has a very theatrical feel.

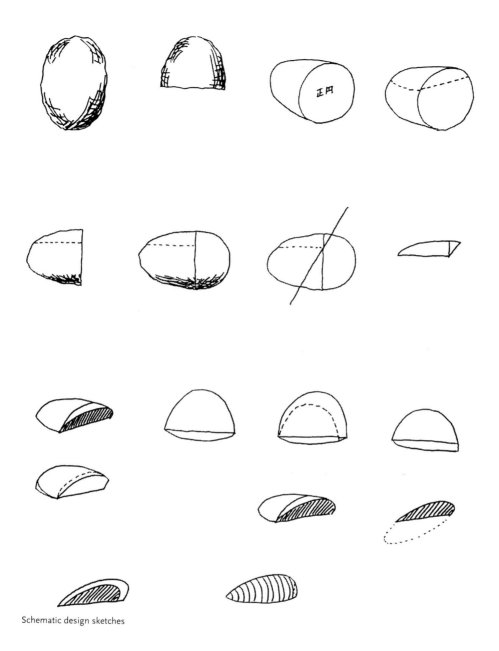

正円

Schematic design sketches

The final structure of the chapel appears to emerge from an oval volume, truncated by various planes. The different volumes build into an irregular space of curved lines.

Location map

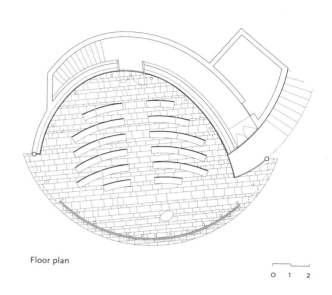

Floor plan

0　1　2

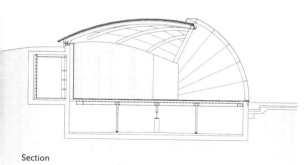

Section

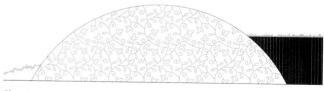

Elevation

CEMETERY IN PONTE BUGGIANESE

Massimo Mariani | Ponte Buggianese, Italy | 2006
© Alessandro Ciampi | Renderings: Alessandro Mariani

Religion: Catholic

 The expansion project covers an area of 48,440 sq ft next to the existing cemetery to the west. The plan also affects the southern part, where there is a side entrance. Plans have been designed for 1,230 niches, 12 private mortuary chapels and 720 spaces for ossuaries and funeral urns. The lack of homogeneity among the already-constructed buildings — which mainly date from the 19th century and the 1960s — creates a type of architectural confusion and causes the cemetery a loss of identity.

A longitudinal axis crosses the site to connect the main entrance with the church, while a horizontal axis unites the side entrances. The project involved demolishing the old church which obstructed access to the expansion. The new church, at the end of the longitudinal axis, is characterized by large crosses on each side, which function as iconographic and structural elements. The other parts of the church were made from glass, in a way that appears to fit inside the stones that cover the chapel area.

Two reinforced white concrete volumes stand on either side of the church, following the perimeter of the cemetery and featuring a large platform which creates a shady area. These buildings have two floors. The ground floor houses the different spaces for the ossuaries and funeral urns, as well as chairs, toilets, fountains and prayer spaces. The first floor, which has a balcony, is where the niches are. A line of cypress trees surrounds the site and helps identify it as a cemetery.

PROSPETTO DI CHIUSURA

CIPRESSI

VETRO

LA CROCE STRUTTURALE IN MURATURA

CAPRIATE C.A

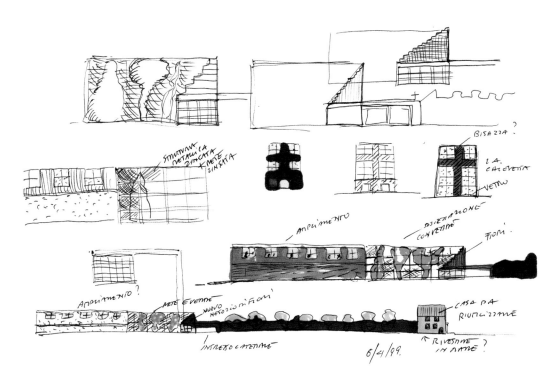

STRUTTURA METALLICA ZINCATA E RETE ZINCATA

BISAZZA ?

LA CROCETTA

VETRO

AMPLIAMENTO

PSISTEMAZIONE COPERTINE

FIORI

AMPLIAMENTO ?

RETE EVENTUALE

NUOVO NEGOZIO DI FIORI

CASA DA RIUTILIZZARE

INTREKO LATERIALE

RIVESTIRE IN RAME ?

6/4/99.

Sketches

^ The church, with a large crucifix and glass walls, appears to emerge from the stone-clad building that contains the 12 private chapels.

Render

Sketch

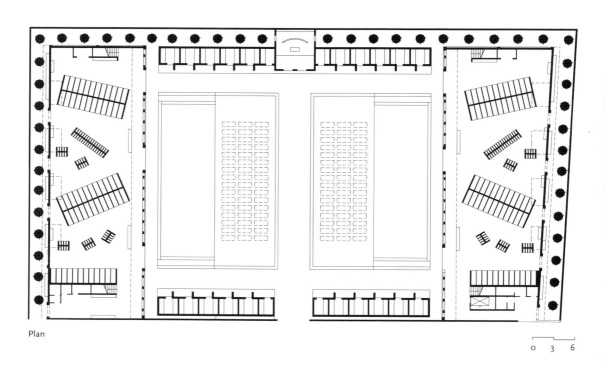

Plan

ders

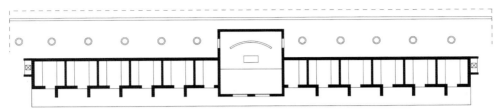

Floor plan of the church and 12 private chapels

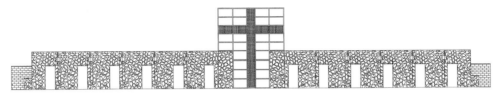

Elevation

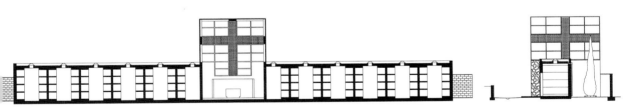

ongitudinal and cross sections

The pattern on the glass creates interesting reflections and shadows inside the church. During the day, the interior lighting changes and generates a heavy spiritual weight.

PARK SYNAGOGUE EAST

Mark Simon (FAIA), Edward J. Keagle (AIA)/Centerbrook Architects and Planners | Pepper Pike, OH, USA | 2006
© Scott Frances

Religion: Judaism

This new-build volume enables the expansion of a campus in Cleveland Heights designed by Eric Mendelsohn in 1950. The new campus incorporates a sanctuary, school and library as well as offering congregants a community center. The building is a simple steel box-shaped structure covered with copper panels. Three large organic forms emerge from this regular structure. One is the Jerusalem stone sanctuary and the others are roofs that protect the entrances to the school, synagogue, the library and offices. These roofs appear to come together like two hands in a gesture of welcome. The double-height vestibule is the main axis of the building. The school wing is located on the eastern side; the sanctuary in the middle, and the other spaces in the west wing.

The synagogue is surrounded outdoors and in by monumental stone walls. The stones are arranged in large horizontal bands that recall the construction of the early temples of Jerusalem. The lighting in the synagogue enters indirectly from four edges and provides a soft glow that generates a feeling of quietude and solace.

Bursting from the back of the bimah is the ark. From it emerges a large curved canopy of interwoven wooden beams. As well as reflecting voices and music, this canopy provides the congregation with a further feeling of protection. Above the ark's canopy is a higher curving ceiling of wooden slats from which a number of small lamps hang and light up like stars at night. While this building is straightforward for the sake of economy, the choice of materials and the lighting have created a sanctuary.

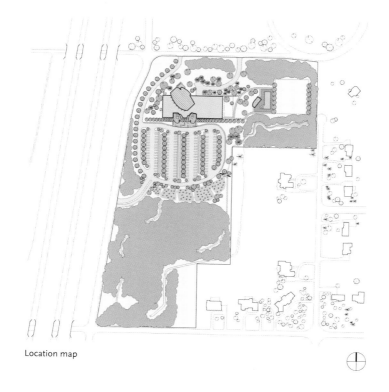

Location map

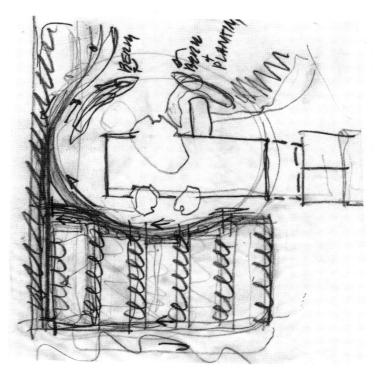

Sketch

∧ Moveable walls make it possible to unify the sanctuary space with adjacent meeting room and social hall to increase the space dedicated to worship on special days.

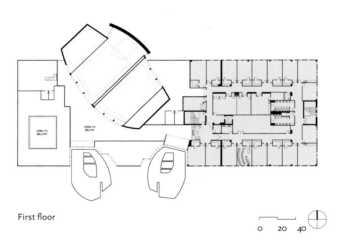

Ground floor

First floor

0   20   40

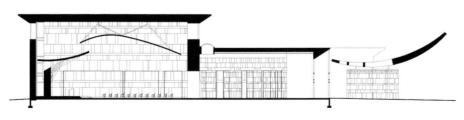

Section

SENDAI BAPTIST CHURCH

Soy Source Architectural Design Office | Kimachi-dori Aoba-ku, Sendai, Japan | 2007
© Hiroshi Yokoyama

Religion: Baptist Church

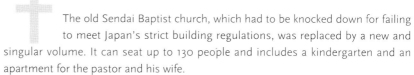 The old Sendai Baptist church, which had to be knocked down for failing to meet Japan's strict building regulations, was replaced by a new and singular volume. It can seat up to 130 people and includes a kindergarten and an apartment for the pastor and his wife.

The new building is located in a fast-growing business district. The Sendai Baptist Church Association feared the current church would be lost among the homogenous new-build constructions around it, so the architects were determined to make it stand out. They decided on a monumental style of architecture to add character to the neighborhood. Although the church, crèche and apartment are grouped together in a single structure, each space has an independent entrance. The faithful meet on Sundays, the kindergarten is open every work day and only the pastor and his wife live in the building on a permanent basis. The top floor is reserved for them.

Inside, red is present on the ceilings, in the kitchens and in the window frames; the warm ambiance is achieved with light bulbs that hang from a double-height ceiling. Courtyards adjacent to the pastor's home create a private exterior space as well as offering views inside the church and to the nursery courtyard. Another of the most important design aspects of the new church is the textures, as different ambiances are established for the faithful and the children. The unequally sized windows on the side wall underline the theatrical nature of the space, and a large horizontal window in the single nave emphasizes the solid character of the church.

The roof tiles of the former church were used on the vestibule floor in the new building. A theatrical note was added by making the entrance deliberately dark and mysterious.

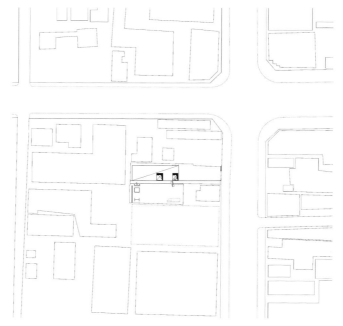

Location map

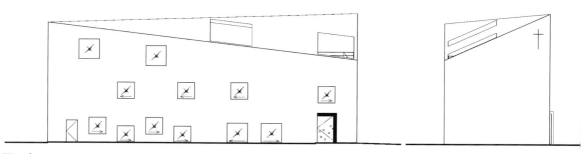

West elevation

South elevation

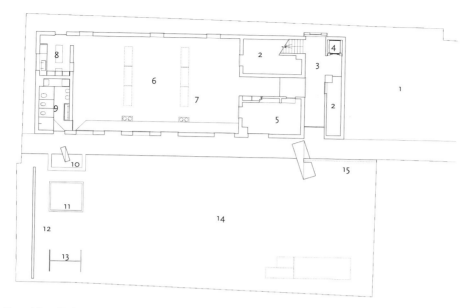

Ground floor: kindergarten and courtyard

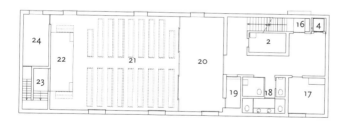

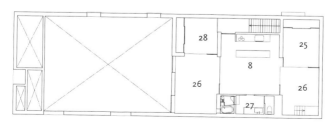

First floor - Second floor

1. Front courtyard
2. Storage room
3. Entrance
4. Elevator
5. Personnel and sick room
6. Classroom
7. Mobile wardrobes
8. Kitchen
9. Children's bath room
10. Foot washing fountain
11. Sand box
12. Soundproofed wall
13. Swing
14. Kindergarten courtyard
15. Security door
16. Church entrance
17. Meeting room
18. Toilets
19. Storeroom
20. Vestibule
21. Chapel
22. Altar
23. Baptism pool
24. Pastor's room
25. Bedroom
26. Roof garden
27. Bath room
28. Studio

0   2   4

∧   When the faithful arrive at the church, on the first floor, they are surprised by the amount of light. A number of simple bulbs generate a warm ar
open space for parishioners.

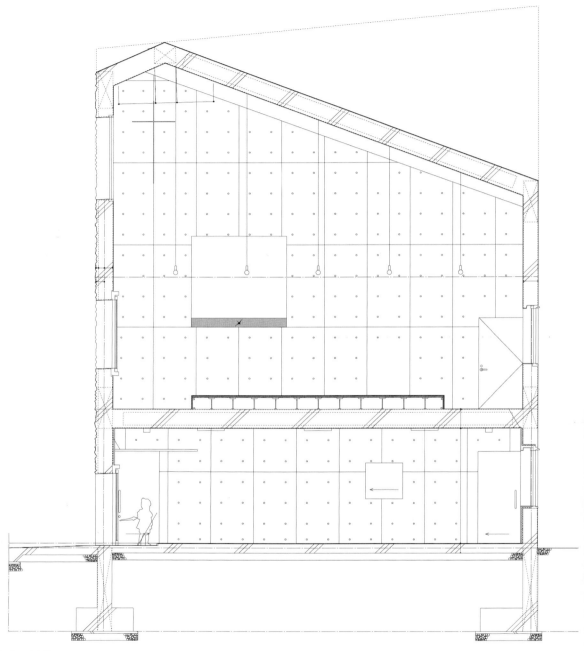

Section detail

Some of the architectural features are repeated throughout the spaces. The pastor's residence also has red tones and a double-height ceiling with light bulbs hanging from it.

Textures give the building a unique style. As well as the rough facade, all the doors and the furniture in the kindergarten have been made from varnished beech plywood.

CHURCH IN RIJSENHOUT

Claus en Kaan Architecten | Rijsenhout, the Netherlands | 2006
© Satoshi Asakawa

Religion: Reformist Church

The new church in the town of Rijsenhout lies close to Schiphol Airport. The location of the previous church, next to the landing runway, was affected by the airport's expansion plans and had to be knocked down. The new building, with facades covered in concrete and natural stone, is located on the same street as the previous church, a long road characterized by a row of buildings close to an important highway intersection. The monumental character of the church is generated by the organization of the volumes and sobriety of the lines, which in this case also convey modernity and dynamism.

The church is aligned with the other buildings on the street and has been divided into three different areas: the church, the meeting rooms and a residence. The three sections fit the morphology of the urban landscape to a tee. They are connected by a large vestibule, a space which connects the passage between the path in front of the church and the parking lot behind it. The architects did not want this parking area to look empty when there were no cars, so it was partially paved and has no lines delimiting the parking spots.

A tall tower distinguishes the church from the nearby buildings. The light inside the rooms is filtered in an original fashion thanks to the play of facade volumes which either protrude or retreat. Behind the altar is a screen of stiff metal cables. Its apparent fragility contrasts with the solid nature of the building. A sculpture by graphic designer Reynold Homan and sculptor Peter Otto was installed on top of the church tower.

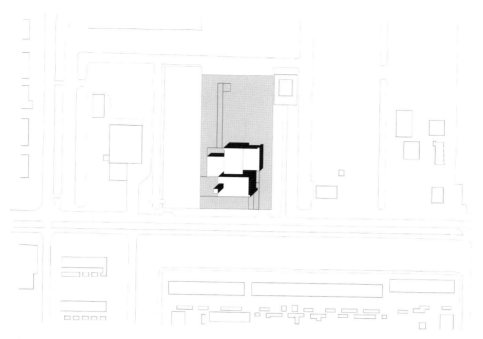

Location map

Floor plan

1. Church
2. Vestibule
3. Church service for children/crèche
4. Meeting room for the church board
5. Garage
6. Facilities
7. Meeting room/archives
8. IT/storage room
9. Kitchen
10. Entrance
11. Chair storage room
12. Storage space
13. Toilets
14. Lounge/kitchen
15. Bedroom

0   2   4

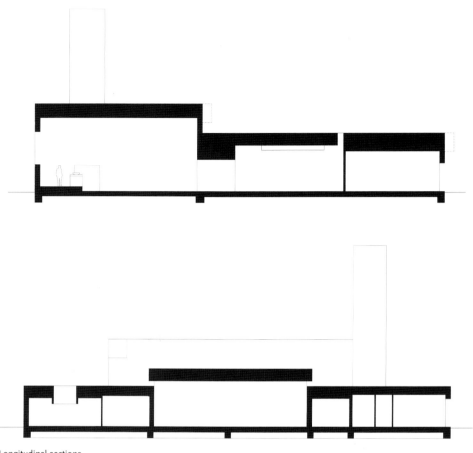

Longitudinal sections

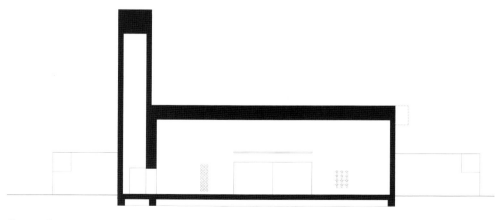

Cross-section

The main vestibule joins the three areas, i.e., church, meeting rooms and residence. The wood on the walls and the carefully designed openings which allow natural light in create a warm and pleasant space.

∧ The church is composed of a single rectangular nave. It can be accessed from inside, via the vestibule, or through a door in the tower which leads outdoors.

PRESBYTERIAN CHURCH OF ENCINO

Douglas Teiger/Abramson Teiger Architects | Encino, CA, USA | 2002
© Richard Barnes Photography

Religion: Presbyterian Church

Work on the first Presbyterian church in Encino began in 1954, following an A-shaped design that featured columns on the inside and a stone covering outside. The architects at Abramson Teiger were contracted to remodel this place of worship. The main goals were to increase the quality of light that enters the church and to develop a way to create a heightened feeling of closeness and a good ambiance for meditation. To that end, the pews were moved closer to the altar, the floor of the presbytery was brought nearer the nave and the height of the latter was lowered to bring the pastor closer to the congregation. Finally, carved planes and volumes where irregularities achieve different light effects and create a unified evocative expression were installed.

The dynamic and changing nature of the light helps parishioners feel the divine grace. Light here is a metaphor of spiritual revelation. The multiple openings create a symphony of light in continual flux. There are three movements: the first, in the narthex, has light filtering from above to produce a sensation of the existence of a space beyond. The second movement corresponds to the main nave: the congregation is lit by large openings to the north, which fill the space with light that represents the love and charity of God. The third movement, the most varied and brilliant, occurs when the light flows directly over the curved surfaces that give shape to the sanctuary.

The vertical cross on the rear wall of the presbytery symbolizes the Resurrected Christ and the love of God. Other elements refer to the robes worn by St. Francis.

The form of the irregular surfaces inside the church is reminiscent of the position of hands praying.

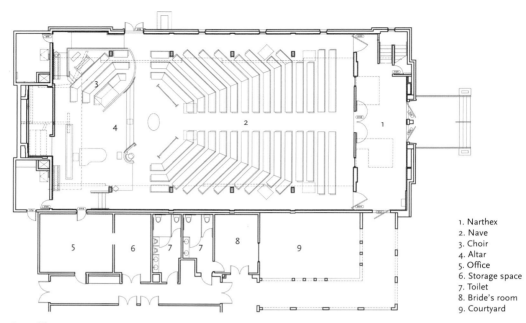

Ground floor

1. Narthex
2. Nave
3. Choir
4. Altar
5. Office
6. Storage space
7. Toilet
8. Bride's room
9. Courtyard

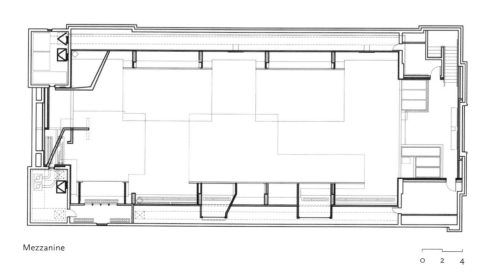

Mezzanine

0 2 4

From the mezzanine one can better observe the shape of the irregular panels and the curve of the pews. All these elements bring the flock closer to the pastor and his message.

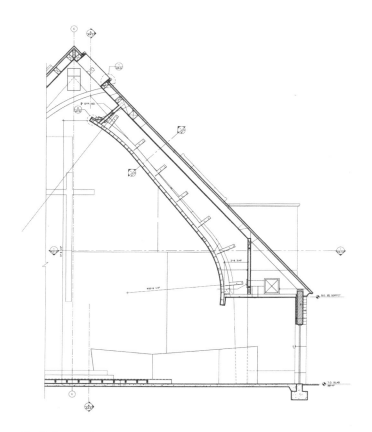

Detail of one section

Sketch of the presbytery

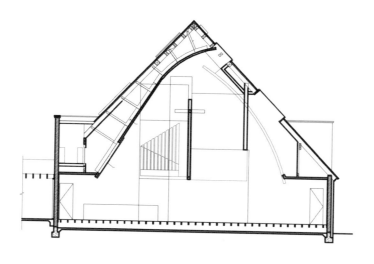

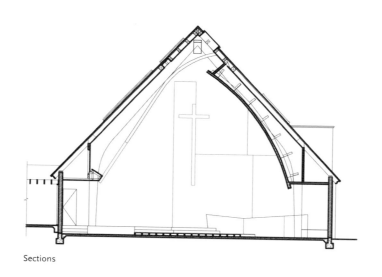

Sections

The sections make it possible to identify some of the openings that produce the intense plays of light that generate a feeling of immense spirituality.

TEMPLE TO CATCH THE HILL

Takaharu & Yui Tezuka/Tezuka Architects | Okurayama, Kanagawa, Japan | 2007
© Katsuhisa Kida | Lighting: Masahide Kakudate/Masahide Kakudate Lighting Architect & Associates

Religion: Shingon Buddhism

This church, built next to the remains of the Kanjo-in Buddhist temple which dates from the Muromachi period (1333–1568), has been designed in accordance with the wishes of various priests. The new building aims to continue the legacy of the Kanjo-in temple that transcended the different sects and functioned as a meeting place for local inhabitants as well as the setting of weddings and funerals. The mountains that serve as a backdrop, the only element which has always remained unchangeable, represent a connection in time between the original temple and the current one.

The building is a simple rectangular volume that steers clear of excess. The interior and exterior covering on the floors, walls and ceiling is made exclusively from selagan batu wood panels. One reason for using wood in the structure is that it is considered a material that becomes increasingly beautiful as time goes on. One of the special features here is that the exterior frames are bigger than the openings in the wall, allowing splendid views from the inside. The architects wanted to dispose of architectural elements associated with the past, as they felt that each age has specific building elements that respond to a particular political and social context, and that reproducing them in the present, without background references, would reduce them to mere decoration.

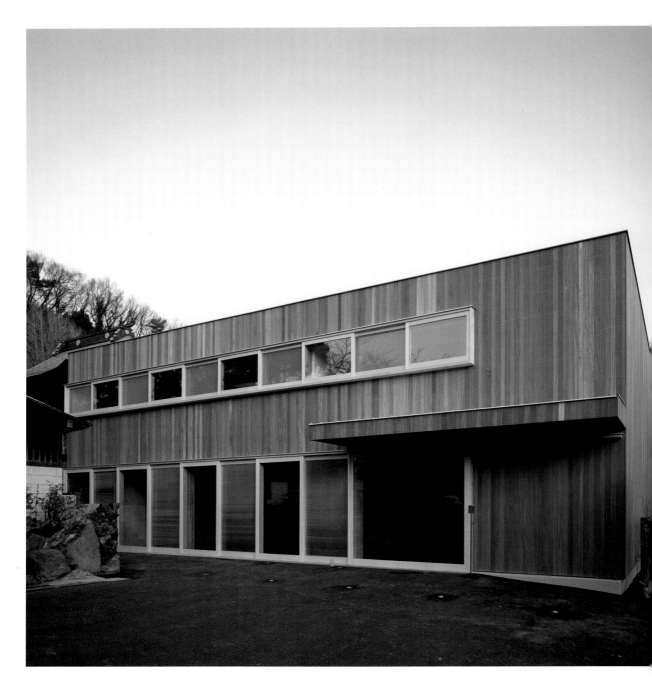

∧   The modern volume contrasts with the design of the old temple. The new space opts for continuity between the areas allocated for meetings a
community ceremonies.

Location map

∧   The simplicity of the structure is continued inside. The only feature of the main room is a large window that frames the views to the mountains.

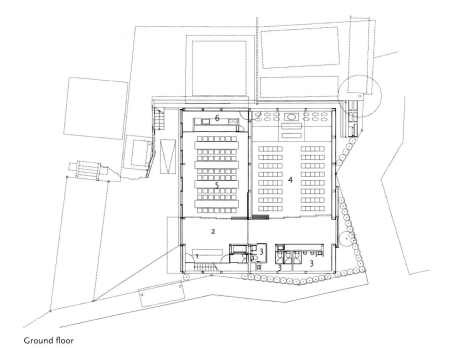

Ground floor

10

First floor

1. Reception
2. Hall
3. Rest room
4. Main hall
5. Meeting room
6. Kitchen
7. Checkroom
8. Reception
9. Priest's living quarters
10. Belfry

0   3   6

The chief priest of the Takamuri-in temple, Tenyo Saitou, attended the opening ceremony. The sutras recited by the monks and the magnificent landscape contribute to a feeling of peace and wellbeing.

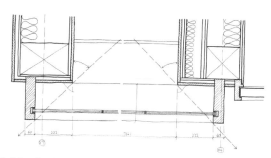

Building details

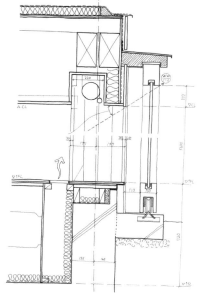

Building details

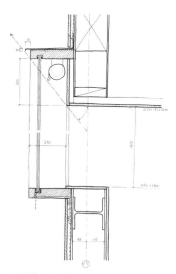

Building details

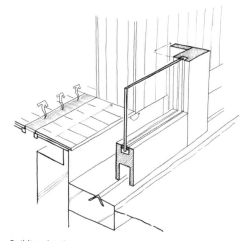

Building detail in axonometry

The details show the insulation elements, the window frames of the temple and some of the materials used, such as the American cypress wood and metal.

SYNAGOGUE IN MUNICH

Wandel Hoefer Lorch | Munich, Germany | 2006
© Roland Halbe/Artur

Religion: Judaism

The Munich Synagogue forms part of an ensemble of three buildings: the Judaism Museum, the community center and the synagogue. The latter two, opened in 2006, were built by the Israeli Religious Community of Munich and Upper Bavaria. The museum, which opened in 2007, is the property of the municipal department of culture. Around 190,000 Jews have moved to Germany from the former Soviet Union since 1989. With this new influx of immigrants, the city's Jewish community decided that, as well as the new synagogue, a new cultural center was needed.

The synagogue symbolizes the rebirth of the Jewish community in Munich. In fact, it carries the name of its predecessor, the Ohel Jakob, and the opening ceremony took place 68 years after the tragic Kristallnacht. The concept the architects worked on in developing the project was based on a natural integration of the ensemble within the structure of the city via a public space. Its public and open nature can be seen by the paths, squares and passageways between the buildings and around the area.

The synagogue is considered the main building. Facing east, it sits on an open space surrounded by a base of closed stone, like a wall, from which a delicate glass and steel construction seems to emerge. The base metaphorically recalls Solomon's temple and acts as a shell that protects the prayer room. The bronze mesh and metal structure allows light to enter the main hall of the synagogue.

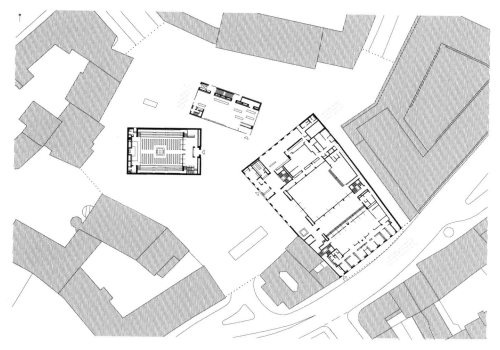

Location map

A travertine stone base surrounds the synagogue. The power of this material contrasts with the lightness and transparency of the metal and glass walls and it seems that the stones protect them.

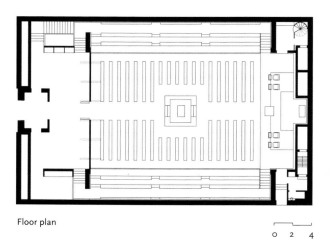

Floor plan

0   2   4

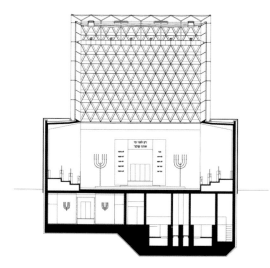

Section

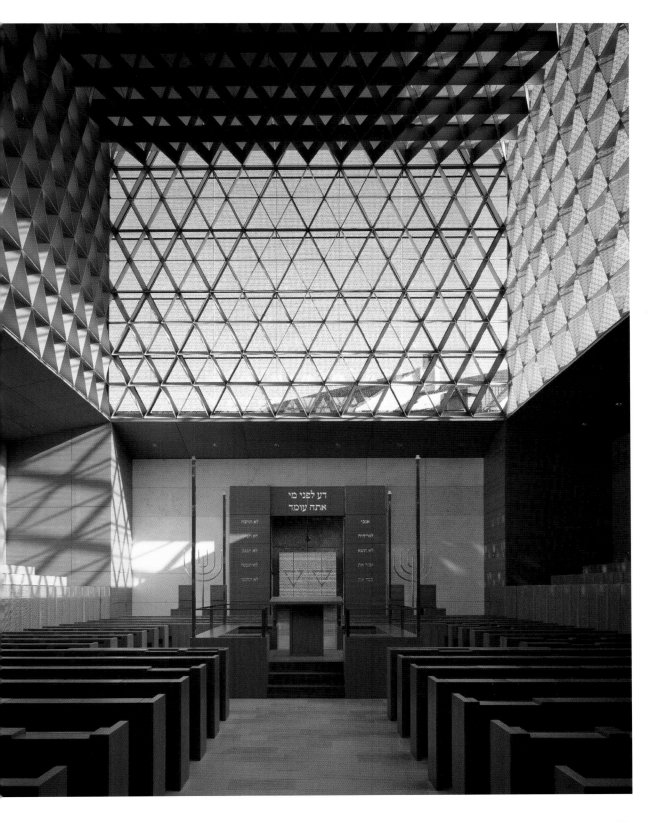

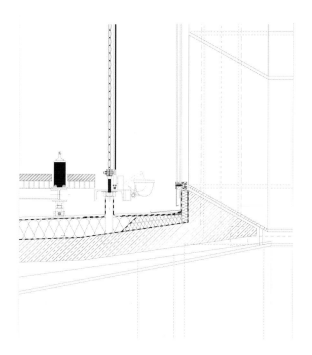

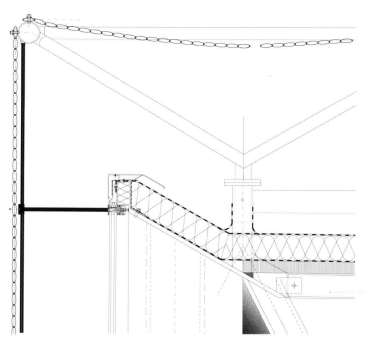

Details of the metal, bronze-mesh and glass structure

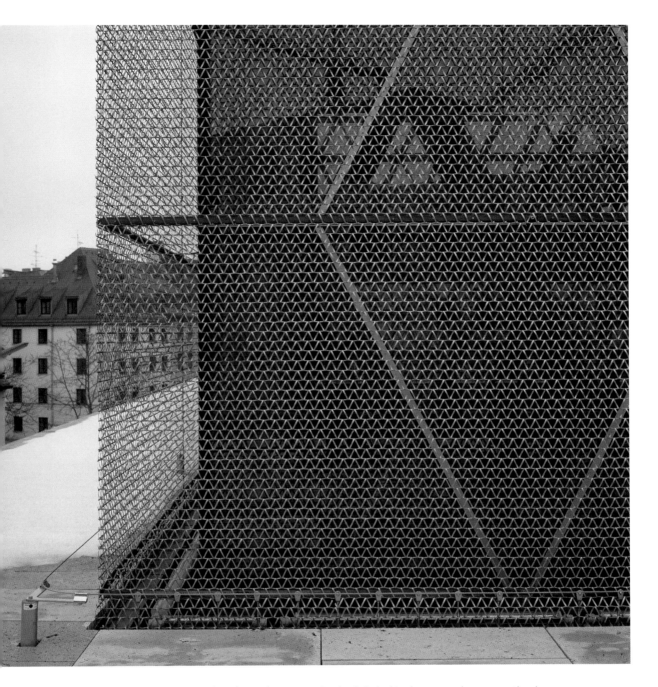

The steel structure made of interconnected equilateral triangles is covered with a light-looking bronze mesh to protect the glass.

DIRECTORY

Abramson Teiger Architects
8924 Lindblade Street
Culver City, CA 90232, USA
T +1 310 838 8998
F +1 310 838 8332
www.abramsonteiger.com
Presbyterian Church of Encino

AREP
163 bis, Av. de Clichy
Impasse Chalabre
75017 Paris, France
T +33 1 56 99 94 90
F +33 1 56 33 02 86
contact@arep.fr
www.arep.fr
Saint François de Molitor Church

Centerbrook Architects and Planners
P. O. Box 955
Centerbrook, 06409 CT, USA
T +1 860 767 0175
F +1 860 767 8719
www.centerbrook.com
Park Synagogue East

Claus en Kaan Architecten
Krijn Taconiskade 444
1087 HW Amsterdam, The Netherlands
T +31 20 626 0379
F +31 20 627 8409
cka@cka.nl
www.clausenkaan.com
Church in Rijsenhout

Emilio Llobat Guarino
Félix Breva 36, bajos
12006 Castellón, Spain
T/F +34 964 236 145
M +34 670 328 262
ellobat@ono.com
New Cemetery in Castellón

F3 Arquitectos
Ernesto Pinto Lagarrigue 156, of. F
Barrio Bellavista, Santiago, Chile
T. +56 2 7350417
contacto@ftres.cl
www.ftres.cl
Fuente Nueva Chapel

Foster & Partners
Riverside Three 22 Hester Road
London SW11 4AN, UK
T +44 20 7738 0455
F +44 20 7738 1107/08
enquiries@fosterandpartners.com
www.fosterandpartners.com
Palace of Peace and Reconciliation

Gregotti Associati
Via Matteo Bandello 20
20123 Milan, Italy
T +39 024 814141
F +39 024 814143
gai.milano@gregottiassociati-link.it
www.gregottiassociati.it
Church in Seveso

Hugo Dworzak
Pestalozziweg 7
6890 Lustenau, Austria
T +43 5577 20706
F +43 5577 20706 15
office@hugodworzak.at
www.hugodworzak.at
Mobile Chapel

Jasarevic Architects
Fuggerstrasse 9
86150 Augsburg, Germany
T +49 821 3434832
F +49 821 3434833
augsburg@b-au.com
www.b-au.com
Islamic Forum

JKMM Architects
Lapinrinne 3
00100 Helsinki, Finland
T +358 9 2522 0700
F +358 9 2522 0710
www.jkmm.fi
Viikki Church

Klein Dytham Architecture
AD Bldg 2F, 1-15-7 Hiroo, Shibuya-ku
Tokyo 150-0012, Japan
T +81 35795 2277
F +81 35795 2276
kda@klein-dytham.com
www.klein-dytham.com
Leaf Chapel

Lamott Architekten
Herdweg 20
70174 Stuttgart, Germany
T +49 711 9979888-0
F +49 711 9979888-9
mail@lamott.de
www.lamott.de
Sacred Heart Parish Center

Lehrer Architects
2140 Hyperion Ave
Los Angeles, 90027-4708 CA, USA
T +1 323 664 4747
F +1 323 664 3566
architect@lehrerarchitects.com
www.lehrerarchitects.com
Bat Yahm Temple